JOBS, HEALTH, AND THE MEANING OF WORK

JOBS, HEALTH, AND THE MEANING OF WORK

MARY DAVIS

The MIT Press
Cambridge, Massachusetts
London, England

The MIT Press would like to thank the anonymous peer reviewers who provided comments on drafts of this book. The generous work of academic experts is essential for establishing the authority and quality of our publications. We acknowledge with gratitude the contributions of these otherwise uncredited readers.

This book was set in Bembo Book MT Pro by New Best-set Typesetters Ltd. Printed and bound in the United States of America.

Library of Congress Cataloging-in-Publication Data

Names: Davis, Mary, 1976- author.
Title: Jobs, health, and the meaning of work / Mary Davis.
Description: Cambridge, Massachusetts : The MIT Press, [2024] | Includes bibliographical
    references and index.
Identifiers: LCCN 2023030566 (print) | LCCN 2023030567 (ebook) |
    ISBN 9780262548694 (paperback) | ISBN 9780262379175 (epub) |
    ISBN 9780262379168 (pdf)
Subjects: LCSH: Employee morale. | Work-life balance. | Employee motivation. |
    Job stress.
Classification: LCC HF5549.5.M6 D38 2024 (print) | LCC HF5549.5.M6 (ebook) |
    DDC 658.3/14—dc23/eng/20230818
LC record available at https://lccn.loc.gov/2023030566
LC ebook record available at https://lccn.loc.gov/2023030567

10 9 8 7 6 5 4 3 2 1

CONTENTS

Why I Am an Economist   vii
Acknowledgments   ix

INTRODUCTION   1

1   GOOD WORK, BAD WORK   11

2   WEALTH, HEALTH, AND HAPPINESS   41

3   RECESSIONS, EMPLOYMENT TRENDS, AND WORKER
WELL-BEING   57

4   MEANINGFUL WORK   73

5   JOB STRESS AND BURNOUT   95

6   JOBS OF THE FUTURE   117

Notes   129
Index   153

WHY I AM AN ECONOMIST

Because e-quil-i-bri-um is the perfect end to Haiku
Because time slows to a discount rate at the asymptote of an hourglass
Because I am color blind to shades of gray
Because I like to tell bedtime stories to a captive audience
Because marginal costs are like shooting stars when it counts
Because there are exactly seven colors in a rainbow
Because self-interest is like a cockroach
Because there is always a right question to the wrong answer
Because my worry lines give me away
Because I approach the limit of creativity but never reach it
Because a rational mind needs a pillow
Because the market for astronauts is too small
Because numbers are like words and functions are like stanzas
Because efficiency is the pay dirt of a lazy mind
Because a fortune cookie told me to "be practical" and so did my
    advisor

ACKNOWLEDGMENTS

I would like to express my sincerest gratitude to the many workers who allowed me to interview them over the years. Without their stories and experiences, the research described in this book would not have been possible. Where appropriate, their names have been changed to protect their privacy, but all other details represent a factual account of the work experiences they shared with me. I would also like to thank my mentor Thomas Smith, professor emeritus at the Harvard School of Public Health, who started me down this research path early in my career. Always generous with his time, he encouraged me to follow the natural scientific curiosity within me and taught me the important skill of learning through listening.

I would also like to thank my friends and family who provided important moral support throughout the process of writing this book, especially Maria Nicolau for sharing all the ups and downs with me over the last year. A very special thanks to my mother, who was my first role model of a working woman during a time when women struggled with recognition and work-life balance. I learned so much from her lessons about how to approach and balance work in my own life. Her generous childcare also made many of the research trips described in this book possible. A sincere thanks to my colleagues at Tufts University and particularly my former dean, Professor Robert Cook, who helped give me the time and space to write this book. Finally, I dedicate this book to my late colleague Professor Shelly Krimsky, whose sage advice allowed me to grow the seeds of many ideas into a single manuscript.

It was a chilly spring morning in the waters off the coast of Southern Maine. Binoculars in hand, I was busy scanning the horizon for commercial fishing vessels operating along the coastline. I was a young researcher at the time and considered myself a hybrid scientist of sorts, working across the fields of labor economics and occupational health. It was 2008 and I was leading a federally funded study investigating how Maine's commercial fishers perceived and managed on-the-job risks. Over a two-year period in the late 2000s, I traversed the water side of the Maine coastline from its southern edge with New Hampshire to the northern tip at the Canadian border, amassing over 250 individual interviews of mostly lobster fishers actively doing their jobs at sea.

It was on that spring day when I met Bob, who, along with many of his peers, would change the way I understood "work" as an essential part of the human experience. My not-so-scientific criteria for including subjects in this study was based on the rigorous sampling strategy—"right place, right time"—and Bob fit the bill. Like many fishers I met during my study, Bob was chatty about his work life despite the intimidating presence of Marine Patrol officers behind me not so casually eyeballing his vessel for violations. The floor of his thirty-foot lobster vessel that was three decades old was a slippery mess of fish guts and entrails, the remnants of bait going into the lobster traps that Bob had been methodically dropping to the ocean floor right before we pulled up beside him. He was working alone that morning on the boat, which was not unusual for him.

Bob was a seventh-generation fisher. He proudly traced the start of his career back to his toddler years, which, at his present age of thirty-four, gave him boasting rights of three decades in the industry. When I asked him to describe the dangerous situations he had faced during his career, Bob did not lack for stories. He had been in accidents where the boat had taken on water and nearly sunk, and his grandfather had died in a fishing-related accident. Rumor had it that his grandfather had a heart attack while working, but there was no way to know because his body was never recovered. And like Bob, he had been fishing alone on that fateful day. Bob shared that he could not swim, which I learned is surprisingly more common for New England fishers than one would think. The human body can only survive mere minutes in the icy cold New England waters, so the argument against learning to swim was more practical than personal for cold water fishers despite drowning as the leading cause of death in fishery accidents nationwide.[1]

Upon visual inspection, Bob's vessel lacked the basic lifesaving equipment required by law. In fact, nearly half of the fishers I interviewed during the study were technically out of compliance with basic safety gear regulations, their vessels lacking various pieces of lifesaving equipment such as survival suits, personal flotation devices, GPS beacons, and life rafts.[2] Not surprisingly, Bob did not shy away from risk in his nonworking daily life either. He was a regular smoker and shunned wearing a seatbelt when he was driving, but he otherwise considered himself a law-abiding citizen.

Based on my conversation with Bob and his self-reported work history recounting accidents and tragedy, I admit that I had a preconceived expectation for his response to my final interview question, which was, "How would you rate the danger of fishing on a scale of 1 to 10, with 10 being the most dangerous?" But Bob surprised the novice researcher in me when he quipped, "Oh, it's not dangerous for me. I'd give it a 3 . . . tops."

Despite Bob's gross underestimation of his own personal risk, the dangers of commercial fishing are quite striking. Year after year, it ranks at the top of the most dangerous jobs in the United States. According to a 2019 Bureau of Labor Statistics (BLS) report, fishing was the number one most dangerous occupation, with over forty times the fatality risk compared to the average US worker.[3] To make matters worse for Bob, research shows that New England fisheries have elevated fatality risks compared to other regions due to extreme weather, cold temperatures, and tidal forces along the rocky coastline.[4] While Bob admitted to being familiar with the harsh statistics of the occupation in general, he simply felt that the risks did not apply to him. It did not matter that his own commercial operation could have been mistaken for a US Coast Guard checklist of the major risk factors for accidents and fatalities: fishing alone, unable to swim, lacking proper safety equipment, and fishing in geographically frigid waters.

At first glance, it might seem that Bob is an oddball of cognitive dissonance among his more logical peers. Not so. Bob's personal experience with his job and perceptions of risk were almost uniformly accepted dogma among the hundreds of other fishers I interviewed. For example, one fisher reported falling overboard twice but trivialized the danger with a 1.5 rating. According to his logic, since he had already survived two falls overboard, his risk of dying was in fact low. I met another fisher who was partially paralyzed from a fishing accident that resulted in a broken neck. His speech was garbled due to the loss of nerve activity on one side of his face, but despite obvious deformity, he also towed the story line—"not for me," he said. All told, fishers described severed fingers and limbs, lost loved ones, near-death experiences, sunken boats, crew members overboard, broken bones, and more. Despite the extreme examples mentioned here, the average risk rating from the 250-plus sample of working fishers was a moderate 5.5 on a 10-point scale.[5] When asked to rate the danger of fishing compared to driving a car, nearly 90 percent voted for the car.

On the surface, the fishers I spoke with seemed to defy a central tenant of economic theory, namely rationality. They ignored the risk insofar as they remained largely ignorant of, and unprepared to, manage a high probability adverse event. They were aware that fishing was generally considered a dangerous industry, but as individuals, they were risk deniers. As I came to realize, my findings were not unique. Past research on fishers showed a pattern of both fatalism and trivialism in response to their personal risk factors.[6]

That made me wonder—what was it that drew fishers so strongly to a profession that could kill them? It is not often a very lucrative career for those who choose it, particularly small independent operators like Bob. Declining fish stocks and increasing government regulations made it unlikely that Bob would be able to pass his trade along to the next generation. So if it wasn't for the money that they would choose such dangerous work, then for what? One thing was clear from my conversation with Bob and others: their very existence was defined by their work as fishers. For Bob, his work was his fate, his identity inseparable from his occupation. He carried on despite the obvious dangers and the not so small probability that his career choice could ultimately end his life, the same way it did for his grandfather.

My research study was about risk perception and safety preparedness, so I did not ask fishers directly about their level of satisfaction with their jobs at the time. But based on the openness of the conversations I had with them and their continued work effort in the fishery despite the dangers it presented, it is safe to say that they identified fully with their profession and derived intense satisfaction from their work, enough so to employ what an economist might consider a rational strategy of trivializing and ignoring the dangers to continue doing what they do without fear. They were simply fishers.

Jobs have been with us since the beginning. In fact, modern humans evolved in direct response to our ability to perform jobs. Toolmakers likely earn the top spot as the first job performed by Homo habilis, which literally translates to "handy man" in a direct nod to their trade. Putting the timeline of the toolmaker in perspective, the earliest stone tools date back millions of years, while the onset of human language is thought to have taken shape over the last few hundred thousand years. That means we were working millions of years before we were talking! Although the nature of work and our relationship with it have drastically evolved since the early toolmaker, the universality of work as an important aspect of the human experience remains.

An important distinction between the work life of the early toolmaker and today's worker is the intermediate role that financial rewards now play as a currency of exchange for work effort. Although compensation need not be explicitly tied to income, that is almost universally the case in the modern-day economy. Interestingly, the word salary is derived from the Latin word *sal* or salt. During much of human history, salt was the universal currency used to pay for goods and services. In other words, salt was money. The reason for salt's elevated status in the ancient world is simple— the human body needs salt to survive, and ancient plant-based diets did not provide enough of it. Salt was added to food as a supplement necessary for the maintenance of life. Although today's developed world diets are rife with salt, deficiency in this essential nutrient is still common in much of the developing world. The root of the word salary is therefore synonymous with survival.

The income generated by a salary is needed to pay for necessities like food, water, shelter, and, yes, salt! But just like an overindulgence in salt, higher income levels do not necessarily translate into improved health, happiness, and well-being. This book will describe constraints on the power of money to impact worker well-being and happiness, especially at higher income levels. The old adage "money buys happiness" may in fact have limits in the real world. Although pulling individuals out of poverty is a universal happiness booster, research around the globe suggests that money's appeal may wane at higher income levels.[7] In regions of the world with strong family and community bonds, the effect of money disappears soon after leaving poverty's grasp, while people in other regions more focused on comparative and material wealth take a bit more money to reach their happiness plateau. A 2023 study finds that the most unhappy among us largely account for these observed income-happiness dynamics, suggesting that happier people may benefit from increases in income more readily than unhappy individuals.[8] All this is to say that salary is an important motivator in choosing work that is ultimately satisfying; however, there is much more to the modern science of jobs than money. Just as there are many other essential nutrients that the human body needs to survive besides salt, there are many aspects of jobs beyond salary that are critical to worker health and well-being.

This book is driven by a desire to understand how work interacts with the health and well-being of the people who do the jobs. Although work is a nearly universal experience, harm and health from work is not evenly distributed across the working population. Each chapter of this book represents its own window into the interdisciplinary science of jobs. Taken together, they provide a panoramic view of how humans interact with work in ways that impact our health, well-being, and sense of purpose in life.

In this book, I string together my own research and those of many other scientists to weave together a story about how work relates to health and well-being and contributes to a sense of meaning in life. I attempt to bring the research together in one conversation around how we choose the work we love or hate, how it makes us healthy or sick, and how it brings our life meaning or makes us miserable. Stories of workers like Bob serve to highlight how the choices we make about work impact our health and ultimately the meaning we derive from our lives. I will also share a bit of my own unique journey through jobs, from convenience store clerk to drug cop to Harvard postdoctoral scientist. As I write this book, I am a college professor and sometimes academic department chair, but I doubt my job journey will end there. I dream of a second "retirement" career that will bring new and unique challenges and opportunities to my golden years. So in some ways, I'm writing this book to educate myself on life's next adventure. But by educating myself, I hope to share the lessons with others seeking jobs that will not only provide balance between work and life but also stimulate the idea of work as a source of health, longevity, and the full expression of life's meaning.

Every discipline in the social sciences, and many in the natural sciences, devote some labor to this topic, each contributing their own patch to an intricate quilt that represents the whole worker experience. Each discipline constructs its own square based on an underlying disciplinary framework that includes established methodologies and ways of thinking about problems that both advance knowledge creation and hinder it when it ignores other perspectives. This siloed approach to studying jobs has resulted in what some have referred to as a "collective myopia."[9] This book approaches the literature from a multidisciplinary perspective to widen the scope of vision in a way that is broadly accessible to academics as well as a more general audience interested in work.

Exploring the topic of jobs is particularly timely given the pandemic's impact on how Americans see their work and how they expect it to contribute to their overall life satisfaction. There is no other way to describe the COVID-19 pandemic than as an upending of the labor economy. The "Great Resignation" predicted by management scientist Anthony Klotz has played out to a large extent, driven by the overwhelming number of workers swapping or looking to change jobs.[10] According to the BLS, current quit rates are statistically and significantly higher than other recent upticks in resignations observed during the Great Recession and the dot-com market bust.[11]

And unlike these other modern examples, the Great Resignation has spread across the whole economy, all US Census regions, and all firm sizes. Undoubtedly, some of these workers are seeking out qualities in work that Bob and his fisher colleagues had already found, which is a job that provides more than just income but also deep identity and meaning. Yet of the nearly 30 percent of US workers expected to transition to new occupations before 2030, the largest migrations are expected for women, less-educated, young, and minority workers.[12] Employment opportunities are shifting as a result of the pandemic, and inequities in the labor market will likely worsen as already disadvantaged groups bear the brunt of this new normal.

Still, other workers have decided to stay in place through the historic transition but have consciously shifted their priorities away from high levels of job performance in favor of the bare minimum. The term "quiet quitting" has been used to describe this phenomenon, a popularized expression of disengagement and a step along the path to burnout. The pandemic has altered the structure of work in so many ways that it will take years to fully unpack the short- and long-term consequences on the health and well-being of workers. This book explores the nascent literature around COVID-related impacts to work, including altered patterns of physical and psychosocial risk factors, and the disparate burden on some groups of workers over others.

The book is divided into chapters that explore various themes within the science of jobs, each chapter taking on a different aspect of how work relates to our well-being. Chapter 1 introduces the characteristics of jobs that promote or impede physical, emotional, and mental well-being. How do workers relate to risky jobs? How do salary and the structure of incentives factor into the equation? Can we identify specific work environment factors associated with adverse occupational health outcomes? How has the pandemic altered these work factors in ways that impede or promote worker health?

Chapter 2 explores the overarching question of what makes people happy. Does money buy happiness? How does job satisfaction contribute to happiness? Are some people or cultures simply predisposed to be happy regardless of money? And how does all of this translate into health and longevity? Against a backdrop of economic theory, this chapter delves into the data to reveal broad trends in the happiness research to better understand the human experience with work and the money earned from it. Chapter 3 then carries this theme a step further to explore macro-level well-being by digging deeper into the relationship between recessions and health as well as related employment variables such as unemployment, self-employment, and unionization trends.

Chapter 4 explores how work can contribute meaning and purpose to life beyond being a means to an end. What are the characteristics of meaningful work? How does the experience of meaningful work change over time, including through retirement? How might changes in the nature of work resulting from the pandemic alter the meaningful work experience? Chapter 5 then brings together the discussions of previous chapters to focus specifically on work-related stress and burnout. How can we trace the physiology of stress to mental, emotional, and physical occupational health outcomes? How has the pattern of stress and burnout shifted as a result of the pandemic?

Chapter 6 concludes by connecting the dots to place the topics covered in this book within the context of the current economy and job market that has taken shape over the COVID era. As a result of the pandemic, the work experience itself is transforming at a record pace. More people are working from home, balancing an unprecedented degree of location freedom against lost opportunities for close contact with their peers. The research described in this book provides a timely baseline for evaluating the paradigm shift brought about by COVID from an interdisciplinary perspective. How might those searching for new jobs and opportunities leverage the existing science of jobs to better position themselves to enjoy the spoils of their labor? This final chapter provides a summary of the major points of the book and identifies future directions for research on the science of jobs in the post-COVID economy.

Much of the research and examples in this book relate explicitly to the US context due to my own experience and education as an academic focusing largely on domestic issues. A notable exception has been my research around worker health in developing world sweatshops. Despite the US focus, an attempt is made to draw on international studies and comparisons where appropriate to broaden the generalizability of the findings across borders. Work is a universal human experience.

Finally, it would be remiss of me not to recognize from the start of this book my own privilege as a source of bias in how I view, interpret, and present the science of jobs. As a White woman born and raised in the United States, I was provided access to a high quality of education from a young age through my adult years. I have never experienced a moment in my life where I was truly without a basic necessity for lack of money, like food or clean water. I worked many minimum wage jobs during my younger years but always with the safety net of my parents. I have worked jobs that would be considered risky or dangerous, and I will draw from those experiences in this book. I have interviewed many working populations at risk, both in person and using survey data, and I do my best to highlight their stories and accurately represent their experiences. Where appropriate, the names of these workers have been changed to protect their privacy, but their stories remain their own. Like all scientists, I strive to present an unbiased and realistic view of how the real-world works, in this case how humans relate to and thrive from work. But I will undoubtedly miss a perspective or underrepresent an important consideration at some point during this book. And for that, I apologize to readers in advance.

GOOD WORK, BAD WORK

It's just a job. Grass grows, birds fly, waves pound the sand. I beat people up.
—Muhammad Ali

A BURNT-OUT COP

Like many soon-to-be college graduates, I approached the last semester of my bachelor's degree without a clue about how to transition to a "real job." My backup plan of continuing straight to graduate school was feeling less and less attractive as I inched closer to graduation. The existential crisis of graduating without a clear purpose made it difficult to focus and complete otherwise routine assignments and term papers.

It was in that somewhat fragile state of mind that I wandered into one of my college's career fairs taking place midafternoon on the wellness center basketball courts. I was there that day for a workout, so was neither dressed nor prepared to put my best foot forward to any prospective employer. I entered the courts that day in my gym clothes and joined my fellow students, most of whom were well-dressed and crowding the center lane recruitment tables for corporate giants like Merrill Lynch and JP Morgan Chase. In an isolated corner of the gym, a portly middle-aged man in a navy-blue uniform was sitting alone, completely ignored by the business-clad hoards angling for their moment with the big firms. I made my way over to say hello to the lonely recruiter, putting aside a knee jerk reaction against jobs that might require me to wear a uniform.

As it turned out, he was there to discuss opportunities in the US Customs Service. After a nice conversation about life opportunities after college, I told the recruiter that my double major in economics and international studies would not be a good fit for the federal agency. The recruiter assured me that they had immediate openings for the job title "import specialist," which admittedly did at least sound like it could be in line with my novice skill set. With some skepticism, I promised the customs officer that I would fill out an application for the import specialist position.

A week or two passed before I got a call back from a human resource officer at Customs asking me, "Are you still interested in the job?" I later learned that the regular wait time for job applicants was on the order of years and not weeks, so this was her standard first question to all prospective applicants upon follow-up. She went on to describe a position in which I would be carrying a gun, patrolling areas of the international ports of entry alone, and arresting smugglers and drug mules along the federal border. I would need to pass a rigorous FBI background check and would be assigned to Miami after training for three months at the federal law enforcement academy in Georgia.

Completely confused at that point, I asked her why an import specialist would have to take on such dangerous tasks, let alone carry a gun. To which she said, "Oh no honey, you've been selected for a drug enforcement position." Huh? My first thought was that somebody accidentally swapped my resume between the import specialist and drug enforcement piles. But this was quickly followed by a second thought . . . that it all sounded kind of exciting. And excitement about the future was exactly what I was missing at that transition moment of my life. I told her I would need a few days to think about it.

I ultimately decided to take that job. I was twenty-two with nothing else on the agenda and no one to take care of, so why not? If nothing else, it was sure to be an adventure. I did not go to college to be a drug cop, but at the same time, I was not really all that interested anymore in what I went to college for. Economics suddenly seemed really dull compared to the prospect of arresting criminals. So, I put on my rose-colored glasses and signed on the dotted line.

Once I was actually in uniform, it did not take long for me to realize that this line of work was not for me. Training at the federal academy was the initial wake-up call. I spent three months at the Federal Law Enforcement Training Center, otherwise known as FLETC, getting killed in almost every virtual and mock scenario they placed me in. It did not matter if I had a partner or was treading into a simulated search or bust solo; the result was always the same. It ended with my simulated death. My education in economics left me woefully unprepared for the instincts I would need to survive in law enforcement. For those split-second decisions, I was too concerned about shooting the wrong person, instead choosing to die time and again rather than face even the smallest chance of making the wrong decision. I did not have the reflexes or confidence in my decision-making skills to quickly make life or death decisions.

On the bright side, I excelled on the tasks that required less time-constrained critical thinking. I was awarded a sharpshooter designation when given time to carefully aim my weapon, I aced every academic test on customs law when given time to prepare, and I could run, jump, and roll on the ground as good as the rest of them. Ironically, I graduated with honors from the Customs Academy despite dying in all but one of the simulated scenarios. I only survived the one because the criminal actor did not show up to the simulation and I was able to "clear" the building unmolested. Despite the gold star on my diploma, I graduated scared and quite unprepared for what lay ahead of me on the job.

Once I was out of training and working in the drug-infested port of Miami, I found myself facing daily dangers that were way out of line with my otherwise risk-averse personality. I was locked inside the prison ward at Jackson Memorial Hospital with drug mules, alone in a narrow cargo hold at the small Opa Locka airfield searching for heroin with a knife-wielding pilot at my back, digging into the stinky bellies of fish whose innards had been swapped out with marijuana bricks, and assisting with the arrest of more smugglers at the Miami airport than I can count. I was amazed at the ingenuity of the drug trade. Who knew that you could turn that white powder into toothpaste? I was nearly assaulted by a woman caught traveling with a suitcase lined with cocaine when I attempted to loosen the handcuffs that she complained were too tight and cutting off her circulation. I would have certainly landed in the hospital or worse if not for the forceful intervention of an astute officer who heard the scuffle from the next room. Fortunately, he had better instincts on the job than I did.

I noticed myself begin to change after a few months on the job. Most obvious to me was that I felt angrier and quicker to become aggressive. My frustration tolerance for stress was worsening as a result of the job; instead of adapting, I was deteriorating. My forced work schedule of frequent doubles and night shifts certainly did not help, and not surprisingly, I was having trouble sleeping. By all accounts, my mental and physical health was beginning to suffer. Ultimately, I lasted less than a year on the job before I recognized a need for change.

Despite my short tenure in law enforcement, the experience was not without many life lessons that stayed with me as I navigated a career in academics and research. It sparked a curiosity in me about how various characteristics of work impact health and well-being. It also very clearly taught me what I did not want to do for work. Dangerous jobs were not for me. Irregular schedules, frequent doubles, and night shifts were not for me. The physically demanding component of the job, carrying a gun, being on my feet all day, none of it was for me. But at the same time, I noticed many of my fellow officers thrived in identical conditions. Many officers handled these same job stressors without an observable impact on their well-being, at least not during the short period I was on the job and able to observe them. Like Bob the fisher, some officers just seemed adaptable to all of the things about law enforcement that to me were health limiting. What I ultimately learned about myself pointed me back toward education, lifelong learning, and an engagement with research around the science of jobs.

RISKY JOBS

Lobster boat captain Christopher Hutchinson and his two-man crew climbed aboard the forty-five-foot vessel *No Limits* and set out to sea in the early dawn hours of November 1, 2014. According to then twenty-six-year-old Hutchinson, the winds were low that morning and the seas were calm. It was a seemingly perfect day to bring their traps to the surface and collect their share of that year's bumper lobster crop.

All morning they pulled up their traps from the ocean floor, emptied them of lobsters, added new bait, and sent them back to the depths. Hutchinson checked the weather at 10:00 a.m., detecting nearby winds of about twenty-five miles per hour. It was definitely an increase over the early morning calm they departed in, but undeterred, they continued on with their work. It was not until they were headed back to shore that things started to go wrong. The winds quickly intensified on that ride home. The boat was hit by a large wave, which put it on a direct collision course for a second wave that blew out the windows and flipped the vessel. Hutchinson himself recounted chaos and confusion in those harrowing moments: "I'm not 100 percent sure what happened next, but the next thing I recall is being in the wheelhouse and the boat is upside down in the water."[1] Hutchinson managed to make it out of the vessel, clinging to life on its capsized bottom still poking above the water's surface. His screams to locate his crew—twenty-seven-year-old Tom Hammond and fifteen-year-old Tyler Sawyer—were met with silence. He never saw or heard either of them again.

It is possible that Tom and Tyler went for the safety suits that were stored improperly in the bulkhead after the first wave hit, trapping them down below when the second wave capsized the vessel. We will never know. Fortunately for Hutchinson, the boat's emergency beacon and life raft deployed as they were designed to with a sinking, providing shelter and alerting the Coast Guard to the emergency. He set off the flares stored in the life raft to attract a rescue in what at that point had become treacherous waters. So dangerous in fact that the Maine Marine Patrol vessel initially sent to search for them had to turn around in fear of their own safety among tumultuous seas. Ultimately, Hutchinson was rescued by a Jayhawk helicopter later in the afternoon sent up from the Cape Cod Air Station. After an exhaustive seventeen-hour search over 130 square miles of ocean, the Coast Guard gave up on locating the missing crew. Tom and Tyler were never found. Upon rescue, Hutchinson said "I've never seen the wind and seas pick up so fast."

Fishing is inherently a risky business. Although on-the-job fatality risk for this physically demanding job has declined over time, the persistence of fishing in the unenviable top spot suggests that this is not an occupation that will ever be 100 percent safe. For New England fishers, the cold waters represent an added danger as the human body can only withstand minutes in the water before succumbing to hypothermia.[2] Part of the risk can be mitigated through safety precautions, equipment, and training. But the combination of fatigue and Mother Nature can be fatal to even the most experienced and prepared crew. The apparent randomness of some aspects of the fatality risk appears to play a role in many fishers' lack of preparedness for that worst-case scenario; they simply perceive it as out of their hands. In my study of Maine lobster fishers, nearly half of the surveyed vessels lacked the safety equipment required by law[3] and captains consistently underrated their job risks.[4] To further complicate matters, evidence suggests that fishers respond to catch-related environmental regulations by taking more risks as they attempt to remain profitable.[5]

To say that fishing is a profession of risk-loving personalities would be an understatement. The scientific evidence concurs with this idea that workers in general sort themselves into risky versus safe jobs based in part on their personal preferences and demographics.[6] For example, as a group, women workers tend to be more risk averse on average than men with respect to their choice of occupation. Although the most risk-averse demographic of men are single fathers, this group is still more risk loving than the least risk-averse group of female workers, married women without children.

Given the high risks of commercial fishing, Hutchinson's initial recounting of the sinking of *No Limits* to the *Bangor Daily News* leads one to believe that this was yet another unavoidable tragedy among countless others. But time revealed a few gaps in his story that ultimately paint a different picture.

It all started the night before. Hutchinson was coming off a bender, drunk and stoned when he made the decision to take his crew out that morning. He was actively abusing opioids both immediately before leaving the harbor as well as during the voyage. He either ignored or failed to check the weather report that morning before leaving the dock, which was forecasting extreme winds and high seas. He departed in the calm before the storm, a decision that no other vessel captain from the harbor made that day. Hutchinson's impaired choices were directly tied to the loss of his crew. I first became aware of this tragedy when I was contacted by the US Attorney's office to serve as an expert witness on the occupational risks of fishing. But this case never went to trial. After years of back and forth, Hutchinson ultimately pled guilty to charges of seaman's manslaughter in 2019 and was sentenced to four years in prison.[7]

In this case, Hutchinson's reckless behavior directly led to the death of two men. This fishing accident was indeed avoidable. At every turn, a wrong decision was made. He started the morning impaired, failed to check or heed the weather forecast, and continued to work impaired through the day, again failing to heed the weather forecast. *No Limits* was alone on the water that day for a reason. It was not safe.

But in some ways, the cards were stacked against Hutchinson from the beginning. Commercial fishing is rough on the body. Long workdays coupled with hard physical labor increase the risk of workplace accidents and ultimately leave many fishers with chronic pain and musculoskeletal disorders over the long run.[8] Many fishers lack access to employer-sponsored health insurance and as a result do not receive routine care, and untreated injuries can soon become chronic pain. Common treatment for these ailments in the past has included opioid drugs. Unfortunately, one out of ten

Americans prescribed opioids ends up developing an opioid abuse disorder.[9] Regardless of whether Hutchinson was medically treated with opioids first before abusing them, he worked in an industry where opioids were commonly used to treat occupational injuries and stress, both legitimately and illegitimately.

A recent review of opioid-related deaths in Massachusetts between 2011 and 2015 broken down by job category did indeed show higher death rates in workers performing physically demanding blue-collar work.[10] Workers in the farming, fishing, and forestry occupations (more than three-quarters of whom were fishers) had the second highest death rate of all Massachusetts occupational groups second only to construction work, with five times the risk of opioid death compared to the average Massachusetts worker. Elevated rates were also observed in industries with a high rate of injury and illness, among lower-income workers, those with high job insecurity, and workers who lacked paid sick leave.

PERSONAL RISK FACTORS

The story of *No Limits* illustrates the individualized nature of risky jobs. It is tied not only to the job but also to the personal behavior of the worker performing it. Not all risks are created equal, and not all workers respond to these risks and challenges in the same way. Academic research on the topic supports the idea that occupational risks are a function of both the job and the person. Individual worker characteristics are essential to understanding the causal mechanism linking risk with injurious outcomes and represent independent risk factors in and of themselves.[11] For example, age, gender, genetics, health status, and behavioral factors such as smoking, alcohol, and drug abuse represent both independent and modifying risk factors for the tasks and characteristics that make the job risky. A worker can needlessly exacerbate occupational risk in what would otherwise be a safe job by engaging in reckless activity.

The personal factor in risky jobs is not always as stark as the *No Limits* life and death example. Small behavior changes and adaptations can make the difference in health outcomes, especially with respect to harder-to-measure chronic health effects. For example, when I was studying a population of truckers, we monitored air quality inside driver cabs on the road. When driving in dense traffic, air quality levels were better in truck cabs with the windows closed to outdoor air intrusion, that is, as long as the driver was a nonsmoker. Smokers were better off opening their windows regardless of the density of traffic emissions nearby because nothing was worse than the polluted air they were generating as a result of smoking in their cabs.[12] I observed a similar example with musculoskeletal risks in developing world sweatshops. Fatigue mats were available for use by workers who stood for long periods of time, the majority of whom were women. Despite training about proper footwear and the use of fatigue mats to reduce physical strain, the women often wore heels to work. The heels destroyed and rendered the fatigue mats useless as a safety tool and increased the risk of musculoskeletal problems in those workers standing for long periods of time.

TOTAL WORKER HEALTH INITIATIVES

The discipline of industrial hygiene has made tremendous strides in anticipating and identifying workplace hazards as well as developing interventions to improve occupational safety for workers. The typical US worker is significantly safer on the job in today's workplace compared to fifty years ago. The incidence rate of nonfatal injuries and illnesses among private industry workplaces occurred at a rate of 2.8 workers per 100 full-time workers in 2018, down from 10.9 cases in 1972.[13] Worker deaths in America are also down, on average, from about 38 worker deaths per day in 1970 to 15 per day in 2019.[14]

These substantial reductions in physical risk over time have allowed scientists and regulators to evolve toward a more comprehensive approach to evaluating well-being at work beyond the "hurt on the job" mentality. The Total Worker Health umbrella within the National Institute for Occupational Safety and Health recognizes the importance of the larger workplace and organizational context, as well as health promotion efforts, as contributing factors to worker well-being.[15] While the old model of occupational safety and health focused on reducing hazards that were directly connected to work, the Total Worker Health approach redirects efforts toward "work-related" risk factors like compensation, scheduling, work-life balance, and the many psychosocial stressors that impact both the acute and chronic health and well-being of workers.

Moreover, Glorian Sorensen and her colleagues have developed a multi-level systems model to identify the myriad of factors and interrelationships between institutions, policies, and societal forces that influence worker well-being within the Total Worker Health context.[16] Their modeling research places workers within the larger context of their organizations that establish the conditions, policies, and rewards for their work effort. Additionally, workers and organizations in turn both operate within the larger labor market and economy as well as the national and international sociopolitical environment. This comprehensive view of interacting systems and layers of the worker experience is key to developing sustainable policies to promote well-being at work and reduce occupational risks.

COVID RISK IN THE WORKPLACE

Despite significant gains to reduce occupational accidents and injuries for modern-day workers, our understanding of risk in the workplace has been transformed by the COVID pandemic. Once benign jobs now come with serious infectious disease risk. Proximity to others was a leading occupational risk factor during the pandemic. The concept of a frontline worker expanded to include cashiers, grocery store employees, gas station attendants, teachers, and so on, basically any worker who could not work from home. Health-care workers were thrust into the most direct and continuous contact with COVID positive patients, exacerbating their job risks almost overnight. The World Health Organization estimates that approximately 115,000 health-care workers worldwide died from work-related COVID infections between January 2020 and May 2021.[17]

Early data from the BLS estimated that 10 percent of US workers (14.4 million people) worked in jobs that left them exposed to disease or infection at least once per week.[18] Racial disparities in the risk of exposure to COVID are common in the workplace. In particular, Black Americans are more likely to be employed in jobs that place them more frequently in close proximity to others and to work in what are considered essential industries.[19] Fortunately for some, short-term "hazard pay" and rising base wages were provided in exchange for taking on the heightened risks related to COVID exposure. The physical risks and work-related hazards of COVID exposure are likely to continue to linger in the future and disproportionately impact high-touch occupations like the health-care sectors, public safety, and teachers.

In addition to the risk of acute infection, mounting evidence of the lingering effects of long COVID are beginning to shed light on the potential chronic health risk to workers exposed on the job. In a large study of Scottish residents, almost half of those infected with COVID still had not fully recovered six to eighteen months following infection. Persistent COVID symptoms such as breathlessness, chest pain, palpitations, and mental fog impacted the daily activities of sufferers and reduced their quality of life. Women, older adults, and certain minority groups were found to be at increased risk of long COVID.[20]

PAY STRUCTURE AND WORKER HEALTH

For many workers, salary or pay represents the most important consideration among job choices. A recent international survey of workers suggests that one out of five workers rank salary as the most important job attribute, with well over half ranking salary among the top three considerations.[21] The importance of salary varies in different parts of the world, with other important nonwage factors like flexibility, interesting work, job security, and coworker relationships taking the top spots depending on the region.

In economics, the nonwage factors that impact job choices are monetized in a concept known as compensating wage differentials. More concretely defined, compensating wage differentials represent the dollar value associated with both positive and negative job characteristics. Less desirable jobs, so the theory goes, convince workers to do them by offering a wage premium. The compensating wage differential that characterizes these unfavorable aspects of work can be estimated using what economists refer to as a hedonic wage function. The hedonic wage function is an equation that represents the relationship between wages and all of the characteristics that make up a job (both positive and negative).

Although workers often rank absolute income among the highest considerations when choosing a job, how a worker is paid can be just as important as how much in predicting the job's impact on health and well-being. For example, a financial reward for work can be determined based on a set rate such as an hourly wage or annual salary, or it can be benchmarked to the unit of production or service provided by the worker. In the former case, a certain income threshold is guaranteed regardless of worker performance; in the latter scenario, reward is pegged directly to effort and ebbs and flows in proportion to it. Economists call this alternative form of payment performance or incentive pay; it is also known as piece rate or is more narrowly defined as gig pay depending on the industry. No matter the name assigned, the distinguishing feature of this type of work arrangement is that compensation is connected directly to worker effort and the resulting countable units of a product or service delivered.

I first became interested in exploring the relationship between performance pay and worker health while on a research trip to Haiti. It was the year after the devastating 2010 earthquake, and much of Port au Prince was still in extreme disarray. The streets remained blocked by debris and subject to frequent flooding, and piles of concrete blocks left only a vague hint of the past layout of this dense urban environment. I was there to conduct research on occupational risk factors for workers in Haiti's apparel sector. Although the nickname "sweatshop" is frowned upon by owners and managers of developing world apparel factories, these were indeed sweaty shops. Oppressive temperatures combined with high humidity and limitless sunshine are the norm for most of the year in this Caribbean nation. The apparel factories I visited lacked air conditioning on the manufacturing floor, and many were constructed with metal roofs that absorbed and redirected the sun's energy inward to the workspace. Not surprisingly, indoor temperatures in the factories regularly exceeded the blistering outdoor temperatures. And heat was not the only work hazard in these factories. Topping the list of dangers were noise, unsanitary conditions, contaminated food and water, mechanical and cutting hazards, chemical exposures, and infectious disease risks, just to name a few.

As I observed and cataloged the occupational hazards in these sweatshops, I learned that most of these factories in Haiti paid their workers based on productivity. In manufacturing sectors like apparel where output can be explicitly counted, this type of pay is known as piece-rate. The majority of these workers weren't guaranteed a set salary for a day's work but instead were compensated based on the number of garments they produced. The faster they worked, the more money they made. It became clear to me through repeated observations of these factories over the years that many unintended downstream hazards could be directly tied back to the incentive system in place for workers. For example, workers avoided even the simplest of safety protocols if it might slow their pace of work. Anti–needle prick components of sewing machines were disabled, protective gloves were not worn at the cutting tables, and personal protective equipment was not properly used in the chemical spraying stations. Although these safety features were available to workers, many failed to take advantage of them simply because it slowed them down. Ultimately, these workers were forced to make a choice between safety and income, and they were choosing income.

This was not the first time I had observed this sort of trade-off in the workplace, one that pits safety against income. In my study of fishers, only one of the 259 captains I interviewed was wearing a personal flotation device, a critical safety feature akin to handwashing in the medical profession. Falling overboard is a top risk factors for this fishery. Half of falls overboard go unseen by any other crew onboard,[22] and many New England fishers cannot swim. When I asked why they were not using the most important piece of lifesaving equipment available to them, the most common reply was that wearing it got in the way of their work and slowed them down. Like workers in the sweatshops, the pay of these entrepreneurs was dependent directly on their productivity. Slower work meant less income, and they were choosing income.

In the United States, strict manufacturing-based piece rate has been on the decline as the country has transitioned toward a service-based economy. Looking more broadly at performance pay measures, whether that be work in the service or manufacturing sectors, survey data suggests that 10–15 percent of workers in European countries and over 40 percent of workers in the United States are paid based on their own productivity in lieu of a fixed salary.[23] Numbers are more challenging to find for the developing world and depend heavily on the country context, including export sectors and local labor laws. For example, nearly three-quarters of garment workers in Haiti receive a piece-rate wage, while only about one in four garment workers are paid that way in Vietnam.

What sorts of health and well-being challenges arise for workers paid for performance? As it turns out, the list is long. The most convincing and definitive evidence is an increased risk of on-the-job accidents and injuries as workers trade off safety for speed.[24] This is certainly the case in the sweatshop and fishing examples above. The side effect of increased accident and injury risk has been consistently shown across occupations and work settings and is not limited to a handful of special cases. All else equal, faster work reduces attention to safety as well as product and service quality. Performance pay creates an incentive to exert more effort, minimize breaks, take risks, and work longer, all of which can increase worker susceptibility to accidents, injuries, and fatalities.

Beyond the obvious accident risk, performance pay has also been linked to worsening overall physical health,[25] as well as increased emotional and mental distress.[26] Based on the evidence, it is not surprising that the performance pay effect has been detected in body markers of stress and inflammation, ultimately leading to a higher uptake of antidepressant and antianxiety medication and elevated levels of recreational drug and alcohol abuse.[27] Performance pay has also been linked to increased heart rate[28] and absenteeism from work.[29] Put succinctly, a productivity incentive stresses workers out, which manifests in a wide range of physical, mental, and emotional health symptoms. Not surprisingly, the ill effects are more likely to befall vulnerable workers like low-income, female, and minority populations compared to their White male peers.[30]

In addition to the physical and mental strain associated with a faster pace of work, workers paid for performance also face uncertainty regarding the total payout for their efforts compared to salaried work. Pay fluctuates based on worker productivity, but the opportunity to be productive is not entirely up to the worker. Instead, work potential can vary based on many factors that are outside the worker's control. For example, the ability of workers to earn under piece-rate systems in agricultural settings are subject to weather, heat, and yield, all of which are beyond their individual control.[31]

Despite the increased risk of negative health and well-being outcomes linked to performance-based pay, there are also benefits to consider. First off, there is a business case in favor of increased productivity of the labor force under performance pay systems. The revenue-boosting impact of aligning work incentives toward higher production levels and revenue in exchange for higher rewards is largely unquestioned in the economics literature,[32] although the impact of performance pay on overall profits is less straightforward.[33] The ambiguous impact to profits comes from the added costs associated with the implementation of piece-rate pay, both intended and unintended. For example, if the faster pace of work driven by piece-rate pay leads to an increase in mistakes and errors, it pushes up the cost of quality control efforts as well as do-overs in production. Elevated healthcare costs and absenteeism related to the physical and mental strain of the pay system may further erode revenue gains from the faster pace of work.[34] Ultimately, the balance of increased revenue against the added costs and the extent to which performance pay results in profit gains for an organization will be unique to the industry and situation.

Another potential benefit of performance pay systems are that they provide an opportunity for high-skilled workers to increase their earnings above the norm. In fact, piece-rate workers, on average, earn more than their salaried peers within the same job, which is consistent with the idea that a compensating wage differential is incentivizing workers to take on the added risks. Workers sort themselves into these higher-yielding positions in a way similar to the sorting that occurs in risk-loving workers toward risky jobs. The evidence suggests that the increased opportunity for higher wages, especially among high-skilled workers, could ultimately enhance worker well-being and job satisfaction.[35]

Balancing the pros and cons of performance pay over fixed wages will lead to different outcomes depending on the business sector, worker skill level, and standards of safety. In some cases, performance pay might enhance worker well-being through greater control of work effort and reward (particularly for high-skilled and otherwise healthy workers), while in other cases it might put health-limiting stress on the low-skilled workforce.

THE GIG CASE

The rise of online platforms that serve as intermediaries between many modern-day workers and the consumer market has driven significant interest in the relationship between platform-based work and well-being. So-called gig work is like piece-rate in that both compensate workers by productivity as opposed to a salary. For example, piece-rate workers in an apparel factory are paid for each article of clothing produced, while gig pay in ride share work is determined by the number of rides provided to customers. For all intents and purposes, gig pay represents the new piece-rate for developed world service-based economies.

Although significant interest has focused on the gig economy in recent years, including the impact on worker well-being and occupational health, data limitations have presented persistent roadblocks to understanding even the size and scope of the industry. Given the newness of the online platform approach to piece work and the relative independence of its workforce, large-scale data collection efforts have failed to keep pace with the growing sector, leaving a critical knowledge gap on its impact to workers and the overall economy. The BLS sporadically collects data on temporary workers and those with alternative work arrangements like independent contractors, but these data sources are still an imperfect match to gig work and fail to account for workers who perform gig work on the side.

As of May 2017, the BLS estimated that 3.8 percent of US workers were temporary employees in their primary job, down from 4.1 percent in 2005, and 8.6 percent had an alternative work arrangement as either an independent contractor or on-call worker, compared to 9.2 percent in 2005.[36] Smaller-scale data collection projects have attempted to bridge the data gaps over time and to cover the secondary job market. Economists Lawrence Katz and Alan Krueger initially reported a substantial 5 percentage point growth in the gig sector over a ten-year period in their 2015 paper,[37] but they later retracted that conclusion after the release of BLS data in 2017 showed slight declines over that same period.[38] A follow-on survey by the Pew Research Center in 2021 found that 16 percent of the US workforce had reportedly earned money through an online gig platform at some point in their past work history, while 4 percent were currently engaged in gig work, an estimate on par with the most recent BLS findings.[39]

Not surprisingly, the difficulties related to characterizing the size and composition of the workforce have trickled down to the scientific literature focused on the well-being of these workers. Despite these challenges, a literature is emerging linking gig work to both positive and negative well-being effects. To be sure, gig workers are a heterogenous lot. The common feature is that they connect directly with customers and accept payment for services using an online platform, for example, Uber, DoorDash, Instacart, and so on. The majority are considered independent contractors and do not have access to employer-sponsored health care and other benefits from their work with the platform. But beyond that, gig workers can be part or full time, and their work can represent their primary source of income or simply provide a helpful income supplement. Other workers even perform gig work as leisure.

To some workers, gig work is flexible, autonomous, and entrepreneurial. It puts the worker in charge of their own supplemental earnings. But for others, it represents precarious and insecure employment that fails on most accounts to provide a living wage. Juliet Schor and colleagues coined this latter category of workers as platform dependent.[40] According to the Pew Research Center survey, 23 percent of US gig workers are platform dependent, 39 percent do gig work at their leisure for supplemental income, and the rest fall somewhere in between those two extremes.[41] Young, minority, and low-income workers were among the most likely to report gig work as a primary source of income, in other words, to be platform dependent.

Not surprisingly, the health and well-being of gig workers depend substantially on this question of platform dependency. Workers reliant on gig work as a primary source of income are vulnerable to the precarity of their situations—job insecurity, unpredictable work schedules, poor working conditions, and low wages to name a few. In a study of Canadian workers, platform-dependent gig workers reported poorer mental health compared to supplemental platform workers, wage workers, and the self-employed.[42]

FEMINIZATION OF THE WORKFORCE

It is interesting to step back for a moment and place gig work within the historical context of labor trends over the last century. The modern gig economy has its roots in a concept that economists have referred to as the "femininization" of the workforce. Although the number of working women increased dramatically during the second half of the twentieth century, historically, women's paid work was disproportionately part time, precarious, and of relatively low status compared to their male peers. They earned lower wages, had less access to training and upward mobility, had less power at their organizations, and performed a disproportionate share of emotionally draining labor. Continuing throughout much of the 1900s, work opportunities for women took a back seat to what society viewed as their primary source of value—as a wife, mother, and homemaker. Benefits and pay were scarce as women were considered inferior to their male peers and partners.

No doubt, women have made major advancements in the US labor force in the modern economy, but inequities remain. The gender wage gap persists, with women still earning on average 83 cents to every dollar compared to men.[43] Women are more likely than men to work part-time or multiple jobs and continue to be disproportionately represented in emotionally draining service jobs like education and health care.[44] But with women now making up a larger share of the US workforce than men, the oppression associated with what used to be considered women's work has pushed beyond the gender boundary. The changing nature of jobs society-wide, and particularly those supported by the gig-labor-contractor model, share many of the historical characteristics of "women's work"—they are less stable, part-time, low-skill, low-power positions that are people facing and emotionally draining, with limited opportunity for training and advancement.[45] Gig companies can externalize the cost of worker health and well-being by not providing important benefits such as health insurance, leaving little financial incentive for these companies to support and provide a health-promoting work environment to their gig "employees."

It is too soon to know whether the labor market upheaval related to the COVID pandemic will result in significant and long-term changes to how workers are compensated for their effort. However, the upward trend kickstarted by gig work platforms over the last ten years seems likely to get fresh momentum from increased labor mobility in the post-COVID labor market. Companies may capture the gains from this mobility by offering flexibility and remote work options in exchange for employment contracts that tie compensation directly to the amount of work desired by the individual employee. This signals potentially good news to high-skilled, high-paid workers looking to leverage their knowledge and control their work effort, but at the same time, it may disadvantage the low-skilled, low-paid workforce who are most at risk of the ill-health effects of performance-based pay.

WORK ENVIRONMENT AND HEALTH

I was approaching the last hour of a double shift at Miami's international airport terminal after nearly sixteen hours of questioning and searching passengers, punctuated by only a few well-earned breaks in the windowless white-walled room for officers off the terminal floor. Although much of this job was predictably boring, there was nothing predictable about my work schedule. My work time would change week to week with no discernable pattern, and my one day off would rotate with each new schedule. Fresh out of college, I was working fifty-five- to sixty-five-hour weeks as a condition of the job.

Despite the monotony of a typical workday, on any given shift I might encounter a range of challenging situations. There was the regular testosterone-fueled inappropriate water cooler talk from my mostly male colleagues who overestimated their own sense of humor. My male manager often assigned female officers the most repetitive and least desirable tasks because according to him, women were better at them. There was the regular risk of harm from detainees who perceived me as the one thing standing in the way of their freedom, as well as fatigue from standing on my feet all day while attempting to maintain a calm professionalism with grumpy travelers.

Most troubling to me as a new worker was the lack of control I had to make judgments that I perceived as reasonable to the circumstances. Case in point were the myriad of zero-tolerance policies in the 1990s related to pharmaceuticals and drugs that gave me no discretion over my decision to arrest a traveler. I facilitated the arrest of a frail elderly French national who was handcuffed to his wheelchair while awaiting a local police transport to jail because he had reported on his customs declaration (and we subsequently found) his prescription for Rohypnol (aka roofies). Although the medication was legally prescribed by his French physician for medical reasons, the "date rape" drug was banned in the United States for any purpose. It fell under the zero-tolerance, must-arrest guidelines in place at that time in US ports. Although I worked in a high-stress, high-risk setting, I was truly powerless to make rational decisions. I was just an enforcer.

On that particularly long shift in the fall of 1998, and after fifteen hours of nearly continuous work, I reached a peak level of exhaustion that even my twenty-two-year-old body was ill-equipped to manage. I was at a breaking point. I was assigned during the last hour of my shift the routine task of interviewing and searching passengers before they exited the terminal gates. Without much enthusiasm, I asked the next traveler in line to come with me to the search table, which was adjacent to the podium where she was randomly selected for a routine search. The woman offered no eye contact or recognition of my existence, other than to respond with a blatant "No." I repeated my request, which was met with another resounding, "No, I will not. I'm going through." We went back and forth like this a few more times before I felt an anger welling up in me. Who was this woman to treat me like I didn't exist? In that moment of arguing with her, I felt my right arm lift from my side and my fist tighten. My body was moving on instinct, driven by what some psychologists would call my "old brain." In my mind's eye, I hit that woman with my clinched fist, square on the nose.

Fortunately for me and for her that day, a punch to the face was not how this story ended. That brief emotional reaction was replaced by reason. I released my arm and hand back to my side, took a deep breath, told my manager I needed to tap out, and walked away. Never mind that she may have been refusing the search to hide contraband or drugs, it was not worth losing myself to find it. Just the urge to hit someone was evidence I needed to step back and reevaluate my work situation. I did not like the person I had become. I turned in my two weeks' notice a few days later.

Many researchers have explored how various aspects of work initiate or contribute to mental and physical health problems in workers. Although no two workers are the same, we can draw some common themes from the literature about the job characteristics that may negatively impact health, particularly among vulnerable workers. A recent meta-analysis combined the results of previous studies on mental health at work to identify eleven job characteristics likely to result in common mental health problems like anxiety and depression.[46] Although these job characteristics were specifically tied to mental health distress, they can also have direct or downstream consequences on physical health.

Work-related risk factors related to mental health problems:
High job demand
Low job control
Low workplace social support
Reward for work not commensurate with effort required
Insufficient clarity and justice involved in the distribution of resources and
    benefits,
Low level of respect and dignity received from management
Organizational change
Job insecurity
Temporary employment status
Bullying and role stress
Atypical working hours

The first two items in the list, high job demand and low job control, are the primary variables outlined by the well-known job-demand-control model.[47] This model aptly ties mental health strain and worker burnout to the brutal combination of high-stress work environments in which workers lack meaningful power to direct their work destinies. Lack of control over the work schedule and temporal pattern of effort ranks highly among job control concerns. Research suggests that low work schedule control leads to higher levels of musculoskeletal problems[48] and illness-related absenteeism;[49] alternatively, workers with greater control over their work schedules experience less work-life balance conflicts.[50]

High job stress, low job control, and lack of supports were certainly at play for me in my swift burnout as a customs officer. Long periods of boredom were randomly punctuated with moments of elevated stress, and quick decisions were made under the influence of intense fatigue. I had no control over my job tasks or pattern of work. My job was to follow the law and not question or deviate from it.

Additional research has extended the job-demand-control model to include social supports, another job characteristic linked to mental health. The job-demand-control-support model recognizes the role that increased social supports in the workplace might play to moderate the adverse effects of a high-stress and low-control job setting. Certainly, the lack of social supports and a particularly unfavorable atmosphere for female officers made my work in drug enforcement all the more challenging. Other important job characteristics such as scheduling are also thought to represent modifying factors in understanding the job-demand-control model within the context of worker well-being.[51]

Compensation is another significant factor that can strain worker mental health. Specific aspects of the financial reward for work that impact well-being include instances where the salary does not match the effort required or when the process for determining compensation is perceived as unclear or unfair. Respect for worker dignity by management can also impact worker mental health outcomes. Organizational change, particularly when it is accompanied by uncertainties around job security, unclear responsibilities within the organization, or role ambiguities can negatively affect worker mental health.

Temporary employment status, otherwise known as part-time, contingent, or precarious work, has been shown to negatively impact worker health outcomes. In today's economy, there is a growing overlap between workers designated as temporary and those receiving performance pay or gig pay as mentioned previously. To understand the impact that temporary or gig work has on health outcomes, we must first understand what drives a given worker toward these temporary and gig arrangements in the first place. If it is done by choice to increase work-time flexibility, the part-time or gig work can serve the purpose for which it was designed—to generate additional income in the most flexible way and at a level determined by the worker. However, in cases where the part-time or gig work may be taken on by a worker due to a lack of predictable higher-paying, full-time employment, the worker faces a much different risk to their health and well-being.

THE SHIFT CASE

The final job characteristic noted above in the list of factors impacting worker mental health—atypical working hours—can be defined as work performed outside a standard and predictable daytime routine. An atypical work schedule could imply workers on a routine night shift, those on rotating shifts that include day and night effort, or irregular work schedules that vary from week to week in timing and hours worked. In general, any work outside the standard daytime schedule assigned to the "typical" worker could be categorized as atypical. This was certainly one of the factors that most impacted me during my brief stint with Customs. In addition to forced overtime effort and early morning and late-night shifts, my days and hours worked would change week to week and my single day off would rotate. I was not able to develop a consistent out-of-work routine necessary to attend to my own physical and mental health.

Out of all the nonstandard work arrangements related to my own work experience with Customs, night-time effort has been scientifically studied the most. Nearly a third of US workers perform their jobs during the evening and early morning hours, many of whom work regular night shifts. The story is much the same in the European Union, where one in five employees report working nights at least once per month.[52] Health problems associated with night shift work include sleep loss, type 2 diabetes, weight gain, heart disease, and cancer.[53] The evidence of a cancer link is strong enough that the International Agency for Research on Cancer categorizes night shift work as "probably carcinogenic to humans" (Group 2A).[54] In other words, the world's leading medical experts believe there is sufficient evidence to intuit a causal link between working the night shift and certain forms of cancer, including breast, prostate, and colorectal cancer. Danish night shift workers have already leveraged the science to successfully argue for workers' compensation coverage for cancer diagnoses received after many years of night shift work activity.[55] Night shift work has also been linked to poor work quality and increased occupational injuries and accidents.

To understand the causal pathways linking night shift and health outcomes, it is helpful to identify the differences between night shift effort and daytime effort. First off, those who work the night shift have different exposure to light than day shifters, being around more artificial light at night and more darkness during the day. Sun exposure on the skin is a primary mechanism for the uptake of vitamin D in the body, potentially putting night shifters at a nutritional disadvantage relative to their day working peers. They also tend to eat the wrong things at the wrong times, with meals that are more irregular and frequent and poorer diet choices available in the late evening. Late-night eating, which is common among night shifters, has been shown to increase the risk of obesity.[56]

These altered patterns of light exposure and diet can disrupt the body's natural circadian rhythm, resulting in hormone imbalance and nervous system and cardiovascular irregularities, which can impact metabolism and blood pressure as well as disrupt overall body homeostasis. Sleep challenges related to working the night shift can alter the immune response and make the body more vulnerable to infection and inflammation. To make matters worse, workers on the night shift tend to drink more alcohol, smoke more cigarettes, and exercise less on average than standard day workers, leading to their own long list of health conditions related to obesity, inactivity, and poor lifestyle choices.[57]

It is difficult to know which of the many potential negative pathways linking night work to health are impacting any given worker, and it is equally challenging to disentangle the maladaptive personal behaviors from true circadian disruptions. Workers can moderate the impact of night shift by engaging in healthy behaviors, prioritizing healthy diet choices, exercise, and quality sleep habits. Night shift employers can also ease the burden on workers by developing scheduling protocols that provide workers with sufficient downtime to recover and by reducing overtime requirements. Some workers are better adapted physically and mentally to handle the bodily stress associated with night work, and some employers provide the necessary supports to encourage health maintenance in their employees.

Unfortunately, much of the scientific evidence relating night shift to poor health outcomes does not distinguish between the night part of the shift from other nonstandard work-time arrangements. Instead, the categorization of shift work generally lumps together multiple types of nonstandard arrangements, including irregular work scheduling that can include both night and day effort but in an inconsistent pattern. Although the negative health implications of irregular scheduling versus consistent nighttime effort may have similar consequences, they may also impact worker well-being in unique and different ways.

To narrow in on this distinction, I investigated data from a large survey of US workers who reported working night and irregular shift arrangements to distinguish between these two common categorizations of shift work.[58] Interestingly, the biggest and most consistent impact to general worker health came from irregular scheduling and not night shift. Workers whose primary job subjected them to irregular shift work experienced 1.5 times higher odds of reporting poor health compared to workers in standard arrangements. The results were similar for workers who reported a second job with an irregular schedule, and the negative effects compounded and lingered over time. Meanwhile, the night shift only negatively impacted workers in this cohort when it was experienced over a number of years, and even then, the increased odds of poor health outcomes were quite small.

Grouping both night and irregular work into a single binary shift variable provided results consistent with the existing literature on the negative health effects of shift work. But at least for this cohort of US workers, the irregularity of scheduling appeared to be driving the poor health outcomes observed in some workers and not the explicitly night component of the shift. Other researchers have made similar findings when parsing out the individual effects of irregular versus night shift specifically on worker mental health, with irregular shift work showing a greater impact than exclusively night shift work.[59]

Sociologists Daniel Schneider and Kristen Harknett developed the innovative Shift Project to explore the relationship between irregular scheduling and worker well-being in hourly paid service workers. Leveraging data from a large cohort of US workers, they found that schedule uncertainty negatively impacted sleep, psychological well-being, and happiness, primarily through increased work-life conflicts.[60] Follow-up research on the Shift Project related schedule instability to turnover and job dissatisfaction, especially among workers with the most unpredictable schedules,[61] as well as lower subjective well-being and financial insecurity.[62]

Looking at the bigger picture, there are a few reasons why irregular shift work might be particularly damaging to workers. It hits on several of the job factors related to mental health that have been shown in study after study to have negative well-being effects on workers. Irregular scheduling is typically not a choice, reflecting low job control as well as job insecurity. The compensation may also not be comparable to similar work in more standard work arrangements. It also shares some of the negative consequences of the atypical work schedule, including night shift work. Unpredictable work schedules, a hallmark of irregular scheduling, have been shown to exacerbate challenges with work-life balance, such as the ability to schedule appointments and plan nonwork commitments, including those that may be important to health promotion and maintenance.[63] Work-life balance can be particularly problematic among workers with families, where negative work-to-family spillover increases conflict between work and family responsibilities, especially among female workers.[64] The negative impacts of irregular schedules are also heightened among older[65] and low-wage[66] workers.

Gig workers are very likely to have work schedules that fall into the category of atypical work hours, including both irregular and night shifts. These workers often get paid higher rates to work during periods of peak demand, which can occur at irregular intervals and in the evening hours. As such, they are vulnerable to the ill effects of performance pay as well as those related to atypical work hours.

Fortunately, there is growing evidence of potential cost savings to businesses that reduce employee wear and tear around irregular schedules. The retail giant GAP collaborated with researchers across the country to design and test a stable scheduling experiment to determine the extent to which the practice of irregular scheduling was impacting company profits. The results showed that management practices that made sales associates' schedules more predictable and consistent week to week boosted revenue by 7 percent.[67] The stable scheduling intervention also improved self-reported worker sleep quality by 6–8 percent.[68] The results of the experiment were so robust that they pushed GAP to institute permanent changes to their shift scheduling policies and provide more predictability to their employees.

COVID AND REMOTE WORK

According to the US Census Bureau, the number of people in the United States working from home tripled over a two-year period during the pandemic, increasing from 5.7 percent (9 million workers) in 2019 to 17.9

percent (27.6 million workers) in 2021.[69] Nearly one in four workers in Massachusetts now reportedly work from home. One study using pre-pandemic employment data estimated that nearly 40 percent of US jobs could be performed entirely at home, suggesting there is still room to grow toward an even more remote work future for US workers.[70] The predictions on remote work potential are even higher for workers in computer-based office environments, where 70 percent of workers could work from home without losing productivity.[71] The boost in remote work opportunities for US workers post-pandemic have been attributed to demand from workers, investments and innovations in human and physical capital that support the remote work environment, and a lingering infection risk from COVID.

Research on the pros and cons of remote work done before the pandemic showed wide variability across workers. On the plus side, remote work provides more flexibility, reduced commute time, and the potential for better work-life balance, albeit not uniformly enjoyed across all workers. On the downside, remote workers are more isolated from their peers and have reduced access to resources, and may experience ergonomic stressors from poor in-home workstation design. In a meta-analysis of the pre-COVID research, Tammy Allen and colleagues[72] argued that there was a lack of definitive evidence on the relationship between remote work and work-life balance, other than a small positive effect of family-related interference with work. The pre-COVID evidence also suggests that remote work may be positively correlated with job satisfaction, productivity, and reduced stress, although the evidence on job satisfaction is suggestive of a U-shaped relationship and tends to plateau and decline beyond a certain threshold of remote work. Post-COVID evidence on the productivity benefits of hybrid work over either fully in-person or remote work options serves to reinforce the hypothesized nonlinear relationship between worker well-being and level of remoteness.[73]

A post-COVID study of German workers differentiated between remote work that occurred during business hours to remote work outside of regular work hours.[74] The authors found that remote work outside of regular work hours was associated with an increased risk of turnover, poor psychological well-being, and higher work-to-family and family-to-work conflicts, especially among female workers. In contrast, remote work that fell within standard business hours was linked to higher psychological well-being and job satisfaction. A negative exception to remote work opportunities during business hours was that it increased work-to-family conflict, albeit not as significantly as off-hour remote work.

Remote work or not, the nature of our work-related communications has evolved as a result of the pandemic. More meetings, more emails, and a longer workday appear to be the new normal, at least in the short term.[75] Research suggests that the push toward more widespread remote work has altered communication patterns in the workplace. A study of US Microsoft employees compared the connectivity and communication of workers who were already working remote pre-pandemic with those who became remote during the shutdown.[76] In the Microsoft case, the shift to remote work resulted in more siloed communication networks, more asynchronous versus synchronous communication, and less connectivity across units compared to the in-person work environment.

Another recent study identified potential explanations for the communication advantages of in-person work compared to the remote experience. Using a cognitive processing lens, a multicountry lab experiment found evidence that videoconferencing stifled creative idea generation in part because it narrowed the cognitive focus of participants to the video conference screen.[77] The authors suggest that this heightened cognitive focus on the narrow visual field dampened creativity compared to communication and collaboration occurring in a shared physical space. However, the experimental results also found that videoconferencing was actually more efficient for communication focused on selecting an idea to go with from a menu of options. More research in this area is needed, but these initial findings suggest that a hybrid approach might provide the best of both worlds as long as creativity and idea exchange are prioritized during the in-person workdays.

It is clear that more evidence is needed to understand the pros and cons of various types of remote work as well as the winners and losers. Remote jobs tend to pay more,[78] with the greatest benefit to those already in higher income brackets.[79] Women are more likely to work in jobs that can be done remotely and are more highly educated on average than men. This suggests that some of those early pandemic disadvantages balancing work against childcare obligations may turn out to be beneficial in the long-run transition toward greater flexibility around remote work.[80] Although there is a strong argument for flexible work practices in general, critical analyses of the existing literature and the somewhat ambiguous effect to work-life balance, mental health, communication, and creativity suggest that proactive intervention and protective regulatory measures might be warranted in some remote work scenarios.[81]

SUMMARY

This chapter highlights many of the characteristics of work that can sustain or impede health, whether that be mental, emotional, or physical occupational health outcomes. But every worker is unique in their tolerance and aptitude for difficult work, and there is no one-size-fits-all approach to the science of jobs. For example, the danger of risky work depends on not only the job but also the behaviors of the workers who choose to do them. The sinking of *No Limits* is a tragic example of this. Physicality and proximity to others represent a new and evolving occupational hazard, where an acute risk of infection, as well as chronic health impacts related to long COVID, have altered the risk landscape for workers in previously low-risk people-facing occupations.

Work that pays based on effort as opposed to a set salary may be good or bad, depending on the worker. Productivity incentives tend to stress workers out, leading to many downstream consequences on physical, mental, and emotional health. Faster-paced work also tends to increase the risk of on-the-job accidents and injuries. But on the flip side, financial incentives provide the opportunity for highly skilled workers to boost their wages and capture a larger share of their own efficiency.

Gig work represents a growing percentage of the productivity-driven workforce in the United States, although data limitations make it challenging to fully pinpoint the extent of that growth. Depending on whether the worker chooses the gig economy based on their work and income preferences or are forced into it for lack of other options, gig work can be flexible, autonomous, and income enhancing, or precarious, low paid, and emotionally draining. Not surprisingly, the evidence suggests positive well-being effects for workers who choose to supplement their income with gigs, in stark contrast to those considered platform dependent and reliant on gigs as their primary source of income.

Moreover, jobs once historically connected with women before their widescale entry into the labor force—for example, part-time jobs with low pay and status and little chance of upward mobility—have crossed the gender boundaries. The feminization of labor across the gender divide is reflected in this new and growing segment of platform-dependent and contract workers who rely on these jobs to make a living.

Other nonwage aspects of the work environment can impact worker health and well-being in many ways, including mental health. Jobs characterized by high demands and low control provide the strongest evidence of poor health outcomes, while a supportive environment can serve to mitigate some of those negative effects. Other work environment factors that impact worker health include a perceived imbalance between effort and reward; work that is considered unfair or unappreciated; organizational flux, uncertainty, and job insecurity; and temporary and atypical work hours like night and irregular shift work. These and other nonwage work environment characteristics have important downstream consequences on worker health and well-being, but again will vary based on the individual worker and their particular circumstances.

The pandemic has fundamentally shifted the pattern of work for many around the world. It is challenging to distinguish the short-term adjustments from the long-term changes that will become endemic along with the virus. But research suggests that remote work may be here to stay. Many workers have been empowered by the tight labor market and their own leverage to make positive change in their work lives to demand health-promoting work. This includes choosing employment that provides more job control, less stress, better work supports, and, most importantly, a flexible work schedule based on their work-life balance priorities.

During the pandemic, many workers have been squeezed into an even smaller corner of precarious, high-risk, and contract-style work effort. The unreliability of childcare has pushed many parents to base employment decisions on a single criterion as opposed to a balanced approach that considers the range of job characteristics important to their health and well-being. Others have taken on risky jobs against their own personal preferences, while countless others have left the workforce all together. While the expansion of remote work opportunities can represent flexibility, reduced commute time, and better work-life balance, it can also isolate workers from their peers, support networks, and access to resources. Poor home work station setup can increase the ergonomic risks of musculoskeletal strain and back pain. As previously mentioned, initial evidence suggests a U-shaped relationship between remote work and job satisfaction, lending support for hybrid work environments as a potential best of both worlds scenario. Although it is challenging to predict whether the positives of the new work normal will ultimately outweigh the negatives on a population scale, there will clearly be winners and losers in the altered employment landscape that continues to emerge post-pandemic.

WEALTH, HEALTH, AND HAPPINESS

Happiness never lays its finger on its pulse.
—Adam Smith

NATURE VERSUS NURTURE: BORN HAPPY, DIE HAPPY

On September 22, 1930, Mother Superior of the North American Sisters asked every nun who had taken her final vows to write a brief autobiography of her life. This was to be a short project, no more than three hundred words written on a single piece of paper. The nuns were asked to include details such as "place of birth, parentage, interesting and edifying events of childhood, schools attended, influences that led to the convent, religious life, and outstanding events."[1] Of course, these young nuns (on average, twenty-two years old at the time) performed dutifully, some with more descriptive zeal and creativity than others. For example, some sisters stuck strictly to the requested details: "I was born on September 26, 1909, the eldest of seven children, five girls, and two boys. . . . My candidate year was spent in the Motherhouse, teaching Chemistry and Second Year Latin at Notre Dame Institute. With God's grace, I intend to do my best for our Order, for the spread of religion and for my personal sanctification."[2] Other newly minted nuns took more liberty to express their feelings, for example: "God started my life off well by bestowing upon me a grace of inestimable value. . . . The past year which I have spent as a candidate studying at Notre Dame College has been a very happy one. Now I look forward with eager joy to receiving the Holy Habit of Our Lady and to a life of union with Love Divine."[3] It is easy to sense the difference between these two statements: the first nun was all business, while the second nun expressed positivity, gratefulness, and optimism about her life.

These autobiographies were stored in the convent archives for over a half century and would have been lost to dust if not for David Snowdon, a clever epidemiologist and professor at the University of Minnesota. In the early 1990s, Dr. Snowdon unearthed these autobiographies as part of the Nun Study of Aging and Alzheimer's Disease and recruited the nuns who had written them (all born before 1917) from the American School Sisters of Notre Dame.[4] As a uniform population, these nuns were an ideal group to study risk and environmental factors related to aging, mortality, and Alzheimer's disease. They all joined their orders at relatively young ages and lived similar adult lives of low-risk behaviors and abstinence, with uniform experiences in housing security, income, and fertility.

Snowdon's team meticulously ranked the emotional wording and sentences from these early autobiographies, coding them for positive, negative, and neutral statements. They then compared the nuns based on the emotionality of their writing with their health and mortality outcomes later in life, controlling for other important mortality-related factors. The results were astounding. When the nuns were ranked based on their use of positive words and statements and categorized into quartiles, ranging from the happiest 25th percentile to the least happy 25th percentile, an increase in median lifespan by 6.9 years was observed. Table 2.1 below displays the nuns' lifespans ranked by positivity quartile.

Negative and neutral-coded statements in the autobiographies did not have an observable impact on longevity; only the positive statements seemed to matter. Interestingly though, being a better and more descriptive writer did appear to have its own separable effect to increase longevity and lower Alzheimer's disease risk among the nuns studied. On average, and regardless of the positivity of their early autobiographies, these nuns far outlived their contemporaries living non-nun existences. Life expectancy

Table 2.1
Impact of early positivity on longevity

Positive autobiographies	Median age of death
Happiest quartile	93.5 years
Second quartile	90 years
Third quartile	86.8 years
Least happy quartile	86.6 years

Source: Deborah D. Danner, David A. Snowdon, and Wallace V. Friesen, "Positive Emotions in Early Life and Longevity: Findings from the Nun Study," *Journal of Personality and Social Psychology* 80, no. 5 (2001): 804–813.

for a woman born in the United States in 1917 was 54 years,[5] a whopping 32.6 years short of what the least happy twentysomething nun in the 1930s would eventually get.

Why were some nuns more cheerfully optimistic than others? Recent studies on the origins of happiness suggest that about 30–40 percent of human happiness is genetic, while the remaining 60–70 percent is of environmental origin.[6] Advances in genetic sequencing have allowed scientists to pinpoint specific genes associated with happiness as well as genetic markers for mental illnesses like depression and neuroticism that are likely to impact perceived individual happiness.[7] When it comes to the nuns who experienced a similar environment for about seventy years of their lives, the observed differences in longevity related to their early cheerfulness was likely driven by the 30–40 percent biological root of happiness identified by geneticists. By the same token, we might also attribute the substantial differences in life expectancy between the nuns and other non-nun women born in the early 1900s to environmental factors across the two populations experienced during their adult years.

Studies have replicated the happiness-life expectancy link observed in the nuns in other populations around the globe. When people are grouped according to where they fall on the happiness spectrum compared to their peers, the happiest 25 percent of the population live significantly longer than lower-ranking groups.[8] In addition to longevity, a solid body of research on happiness has surfaced over the last few decades connecting it to a wide range of health conditions and diseases as well as physical markers of inflammation and stress that can ultimately lead to disease and ill-health.[9] No doubt, unhappiness is a slippery slope.

Sadler and colleagues also used data on Danish twins to test for a causal relationship between happiness and longevity.[10] They found evidence to support a causal link between happiness and longer lives independent of confounding by genetic and common family environment factors. In short, happier people live longer and healthier lives on average, all things considered.

ECONOMIC THEORIES ON HAPPINESS

Economists have concerned themselves with the idea of happiness for the entirety of the discipline's history. In fact, one could say that modern economics was born as an evaluative science of happiness, albeit well hidden under the cloak of a lesser-known concept called utility. An individual's utility (economist speak for happiness) is shaped by their unique preferences and desires. For example, black jellybeans are my favorite type of candy. As economic theory goes, my utility increases every time I consume another black jellybean. Although more and more black jellybeans make me happier and happier, each additional black jellybean is a little less delicious than the last, a concept known as diminishing marginal utility. Of course, I can't survive on black jellybeans alone, so my overall utility is made up of all the things I want or need that are unique to my tastes. But as with the black jellybeans, my happiness increases the more I consume overall, with each increase a little less impactful than the last.

But ultimately, our consumerist thirst is held in check by our ability to pay the price of all the things we desire, which brings me to the universal currency of value in economics—money or income. In no uncertain terms, the economics construct of happiness is tethered to income. If I had an unlimited amount of money, I would continue to express my whims and binge on black jellybeans in an ever-escalating cycle of greed. But instead, my behavior is moderated by finite income and the price of black jellybeans.

To summarize, the neoclassical view of economic theory provides an income-based measure of happiness outlined by the theoretical concepts of utility and budget constraints universally taught in college economics 101 courses. I can only be as happy as my budget and income permit me to be. As the economic theory goes, money buys happiness. More money is always better, although it contributes to happiness at a decreasing rate as income grows. There are alternative and less mainstream models in economics that do not assume all these consumerist restrictions, but this is the prevailing theory in neoclassical economics and is foundational to modern capitalist markets.

This model of happiness is not in conflict with earlier explanations around genetics versus environmental causes. As it relates to the nature versus nurture debate on happiness, genetics (30–40 percent of happiness) correlates with the underlying utility made up of unique tastes and preferences, while environment (60–70 percent of happiness) is tied to the individual budget constraints made up of income and prices. Ultimately, happiness comes from a confluence of factors around individual preferences and income, whether or not it is described as economic behavior or using the language of genetics.

THE IMPORTANCE OF RATIONALITY

The traditional view of economic decision-making where we are constantly seeking the greatest happiness that money can buy hinges on a critical concept that economists call rationality. Rational choice theory represents the mainstream decision-making strategy whereby self-interested individuals select choices to their greatest benefit. A somewhat cynical and selfish view of human behavior, the assumption of rational behavior provides the basis that allows neoclassical economic theory to predict human behavior and consumption patterns—and by default, our previous conclusion that money buys happiness.

Not surprisingly, a growing number of economists eschew the neoclassical interpretation of decision theory and rationality in favor of a more nuanced approach that accounts not only for that ideal predictable behavior but also actual real-world behavior. The fast-growing field of behavioral economics deviates from the law of rationality to support a more empirically based interpretation of irrational choices. Dan Ariely, a well-known behavioral economist at Duke University, points out that people rarely conform strictly to the rational models of economic theory; instead, they regularly depart from that ideal in systematic ways, and we need only observe the repeating pattern of behavior to predict what in standard economic models would be considered unpredictable.[11]

How might economic theory explain Bob the fisher's decision to take on dangerous work? Rational choice theory suggests that Bob will selfishly consider his own best interests to maximize his resources and happiness. Presumably, he receives a premium to do the risky work compared to safer jobs, that compensating wage differential referred to in chapter 1. Despite the potential wage premium, the income generated by fishing is highly variable and uncertain from one season to the next. Research shows that risk-loving fishers make more money than risk-averse fishers,[12] so it makes sense that Bob survives in this profession in part due his adventurous and risk-loving work ethic. Other very reasonable factors that Bob might have considered when deciding to be a fisher like his father and grandfather before him are the deep base of community and family support for fishers in coastal Maine, the flexibility of being his own boss, and the lack of investment in formal education needed to become a fisher. All of these pros of the job as well as the wage premium outweigh the occupational risk for a risk-loving fisher like Bob. He in fact made a rational choice to become a fisher despite the obvious risks.

Although his choice of profession may be rational based on the factors identified above, classical economic theory cannot easily explain why Bob downplays and ignores the risky nature of his work. Bob's connection to fishing shares a common thread among many fishers, especially in coastal Maine. There is a rich cultural history and family tradition of fishing, with shared social and cultural norms that impact how these fishers perceive the interconnections between work, life, and health.[13] All the fishers that I interviewed were aware of the accident and fatality statistics that place fishing among the most dangerous occupations in America. And the vast majority of fishers could describe an accident or close call for themselves or their kin. Yet when asked to apply the risk to their own fishing activities and rate their personal risk on a scale of 1 to 10, they consistently rated it as average (5.5 on a 10-point scale for the group of lobster fishers like Bob). Over 40 percent of the sample of fishers did not have the basic safety equipment and training required by law on board their vessels.[14] Despite recognizing the risk existed, acknowledging the statistical facts, and having experience with accidents, injuries, and death, these fishers rated their personal risk on par with a "regular job." Bob and his peers were predictably irrational in their shared belief that the dangerous occupation was not dangerous for them.

From a psychology and behavioral economics perspective, the lack of risk recognition may be due in part to occupation-specific learned helplessness, where repeated exposure to trauma generates a sense of inevitability and a perceived lack of control. In fact, commercial fishing research suggests that routine experiences with close calls and peer fatalities may lead to a fatalistic attitude about the job and a propensity to trivialize the risk.[15] A common theme among the fishers that I interviewed was the belief that no level of safety or preparedness would save them from fate. Despite the evidence that lifesaving equipment and procedures do in fact save lives, fishers favored an approach of "common sense" over preparation as a means of staying safe on the job.[16]

MEASURING HAPPINESS

So far, I have used the term happiness in the broadest sense to encompass the range of positive emotions and experiences one might have in life. However, the academic literature takes a much more nuanced view of happiness, breaking it down into three separate and subjectively measurable components. The first is affective well-being, sometimes referred to as hedonic well-being, that includes both positive and negative experiences such as pleasure, cheerfulness, sadness, and pain often associated with day-to-day emotions and mood. This is what the nuns expressed in their early autobiographies. The second part of happiness is described as evaluative well-being, more commonly referred to as life satisfaction. This second construct is often derived from questions that ask people how satisfied they are with their lives in general, while affective well-being measures responses to questions about how often respondents felt a particular positive or negative emotion in the recent past. A third happiness construct, known as eudaemonic well-being, relates to one's sense of meaning or purpose in life. I will come back to eudaemonic well-being in chapter 4, focusing for now on affective and evaluative measures of well-being.

Measures of mood and life satisfaction can be seen, to some extent, as overlapping concepts. In other words, a person who is generally cheerful with high positive affect might also be expected to report a high level of life satisfaction and vice versa. However, while these two happiness measures tend to be positively correlated on average, they do not always move hand in hand. Think for a moment of all the people you know, especially those you have come into contact with in the workplace. I am sure you could point to many examples of highly accomplished individuals who might score high on life satisfaction based on their long list of achievements but at the same time are generally miserable human beings in their day-to-day existence. There are also those who achieve great success in life yet suffer from mental illness that corresponds with high negative affect. Abraham Lincoln, arguably the most important president in US history, famously suffered from, and received treatment for, "melancholia," more commonly known as clinical depression today. Frequent bouts with intense sadness would have most certainly reflected poorly for Lincoln in the fluctuations of his mood day to day while his overall life satisfaction with respect to his achievements and status remained high.

DOES MONEY REALLY BUY HAPPINESS?

To determine whether the economic utility theory version of happiness aligns with reality, we have to turn to the empirical evidence. In 1974, Richard Easterlin published an article on economic growth and happiness describing what would eventually become known as the Easterlin Paradox.[17] Easterlin observed what one would expect based on the economic theory: wealthier individuals were comparatively happier than less wealthy individuals. He made similar observations comparing groups or countries of people; those with more money were happier than groups and countries with less money. However, a notable conclusion he drew from the data available at the time was that increases in wealth over time didn't seem to result in increases in happiness, at least not to the extent that one would assume if money buys happiness. Put a bit differently, average happiness levels did not seem to keep up with proportional increases in income; long-term growth appeared to be a wash. Countries were getting monetarily richer and richer by all observable income measures but reported that happiness levels remained stagnant.

Figure 2.1 illustrates the hypothetical paradox viewed over three distinct time periods with significant income growth. Although the expected cross-sectional relationship between income and happiness is observed in each time period (wealthier individuals are happier than those with less money), increasing economic growth over time does not measurably impact average happiness, which instead remains relatively flat.

Since Easterlin first raised this issue, economists have volleyed back and forth between support for and opposition to the original paradox, and some would say it remains an open question. Results linking money with happiness vary based on how the question is framed, which measure of happiness

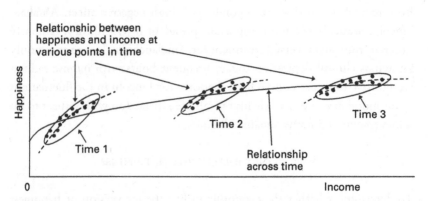

Figure 2.1
Relationship between happiness and income over time.

is used, and the countries and time periods examined.[18] The relationship between money and happiness appears to be particularly stark and steep at the lowest income levels, suggesting that gains in happiness coming out of poverty are the most substantial across the income spectrum. However, the relationship between money and happiness begins to taper off as income grows and eventually flattens out or saturates at higher income levels.

This observed plateau or saturation point after which more money no longer seems to have an impact on happiness varies based on how happiness is measured (mood or life satisfaction) as well as the time and place of the study. Daniel Kahneman and Angus Deaton illustrate the saturation point quite nicely for the US population, using survey data from the Gallup-Healthways Well-Being Index.[19] They noted that affective well-being or mood was positively related to income up until about $75,000 year at the time (approximately $100,000 in 2022 dollars). After that point, more money was not associated with increased positive affect or better mood; the relationship instead went flat. In other words, people were about as happy as they were going to be in their day-to-day life experiences once that income plateau had been achieved. The authors did not observe a similar saturation point for life satisfaction.

A recent study by Matthew Killingsworth challenged the prevailing narrative of the income-happiness plateau with updated real-time data from a large sample of US adults.[20] Using this new sampling approach, neither mood nor life satisfaction plateaued at higher income levels and instead continued to rise over observable increases in income. To settle the dispute, Kahneman and Killingsworth teamed up to reinvestigate the merit of their opposing findings.[21] Using their combined forces to reinterpret the real-time data, they reached the conclusion that the threshold theory of income and happiness does indeed hold but only for the most unhappy among us: the least happy 15 percent of the population experiences increased happiness with income up to a threshold of about $100,000 (in 2022 dollars) but then abruptly levels off, with no further increases in happiness as income grows. In contrast, the happiest 15 percent of the population experiences the standard increase in happiness with income up to the same $100,000 threshold, but the trend accelerates beyond that point. Ultimately, this new evidence of income and happiness in the United States suggests that happier people may benefit from increases in income more readily than unhappy people.

Table 2.2
Income required to be happy in various parts of the world

Region	Life satisfaction plateau	Everyday happiness plateau
Global	$95,000	$60,000
Australia/New Zealand	$125,000	$50,000
Middle East/North Africa	$115,000	$110,000
East Asia	$110,000	$60,000
North America	$105,000	$65,000
Western Europe	$100,000	$50,000
Southeast Asia	$70,000	N/A
Eastern Europe	$45,000	$35,000
Sub-Saharan Africa	$40,000	$35,000
Latin America/Caribbean	$35,000	$30,000

Source: Andrew T. Jebb, Louis Tay, Ed Diener, and Shigehiro Oishi, "Happiness, Income Satiation, and Turning Points around the World," *Nature Human Behaviour* 2 (2018): 33–38. Data presented from original study in 2016 dollars.

Evidence from a larger sample of the global population using 2016 data from the Gallup World Poll identified a global average plateau for mood of around $60,000 ($71,000 in 2022 dollars) and life evaluation of around $95,000 (nearly $113,000 in 2022 dollars).[22] Table 2.2 shows considerable variability in where that income plateau occurs for mood and life satisfaction based on the region of the world. The amount of money needed to be happy is highest in the most developed regions of the world, while the lowest plateau points are observed in Eastern Europe, sub-Saharan Africa, and Latin America. Notably, it takes less money to be happy in your day-to-day experiences than it takes to be satisfied with your life overall.

Additional research in Latin America on the underlying causes of happiness in that region highlights a few major differences compared to the rest of the world that might explain their ranking in the above results, most notably a greater emphasis on social networks as a determinant of happiness. Family and friendships rank higher than health, employment, or personal assets in terms of impact on happiness in that part of the world.[23] Not surprisingly, a common saying in some Latin American countries showcases this tradition: *mejor tener amigos que plata* (better to have friends than money).

Despite varying plateau points and opinions on the Easterlin Paradox, one result stands out in the happiness literature as an unequivocal truth—poverty, and particularly high rates of abject poverty where basic needs are not met, makes people unhappy. No matter the context, happiness improves as people are pulled out of poverty, whether we observe people within countries, across countries, or over time. The relationship between income and happiness is the strongest and the steepest at the lowest income levels. Put in terms of policy impacts, if the goal is to affect the biggest possible change in happiness across a population, pulling individuals out of poverty is the way to go. This would unequivocally increase average happiness levels of a population, while similar income boosts to middle- and high-income classes would have a lesser impact on happiness, particularly for income levels beyond a plateau point if in fact one exists.

So what makes happiness so elusive at higher income levels? Beyond income, evidence suggests that happiness is impacted by factors that underly the framework of societies in which people live, including inequality, institutions, safety, and security. Individual differences also trend significantly with happiness such as marital status and health, and happiness dips in tandem with the quintessential midlife crises of the forties.[24] Researchers have described the postpoverty relationship between income and happiness as a "hedonic treadmill," a vicious cycle where "you have to keep running in order that your happiness stand still."[25] This idea of the hedonic treadmill is rooted in the psychological concepts of adaptation and habituation. Happiness rises with income but so does one's expectation for happiness, hence the analogy of running in place. Predictability factors heavily into our ability to adapt to negative outcomes.[26]

The tension that keeps us on this proverbial treadmill is our tendency to value relative as opposed to absolute improvements in our status and income as key to happiness. As it turns out, our wants, desires, preferences, and tastes are not fixed but instead depend heavily on how we rank ourselves against those around us.[27] Some economists have argued that this warrants a rethink of mainstream utility models that view consumer preferences in absolute as opposed to relative terms.[28] Traditional models are based on the underlying assumption that individuals derive utility (i.e. happiness) from their own consumption, but these same models fail to account for the larger context of consumption by peers despite overwhelming evidence to suggest that these comparisons matter. Early economist John S.

Mill summarized it succinctly when he said, "men do not desire to be rich, but richer than other men."

The ability to manage expectations, avoid relative comparisons, and be resilient to change are critical to getting off the hedonic treadmill. Evidence suggests that we must adapt our expectations downward when dealing with unexpected difficulties and challenges to preserve our happiness in the same way that we adapt our expectations upward in response to positive events. Social media presents a unique challenge in this regard as we now have continuous and instantaneous access to the self-reported well-being of our peers as a comparison point.

JOB SATISFACTION AND HAPPINESS

Around the same time that research on happiness and the Easterlin Paradox made its debut, economists like Richard Freeman and George Borjas were developing a similar line of inquiry on job satisfaction as a subdomain of happiness specific to the workplace. Their early contributions emphasized the importance of job satisfaction in employment mobility and turnover as well as the relationship between job satisfaction and work-related variables such as unionization.[29]

Although this text will often revisit and reflect on measures of job satisfaction in relation to worker well-being, it is worth emphasizing some of the important trends here. No doubt, some workers are naturally prone to enjoy higher levels of job satisfaction than others despite similar circumstances. For example, individual personality traits like conscientiousness can contribute to a feeling of contentment at work.[30] Gender, age, wages, and education also impact the likelihood of experiencing job satisfaction. Notably, job satisfaction tends to follow a U-shaped pattern with age, with the trough (worst period) occurring around the early thirties.[31] Exogenous factors can also impact job satisfaction, which can vary week to week and even day to day. There is some traction in the literature behind the concept of the "Monday blues," with satisfaction trending lowest toward the beginning of the work week, all else equal.[32] Job satisfaction also tends to be higher for employees in smaller organizations compared to larger ones.[33]

A meta-analysis of the job satisfaction literature provides evidence of a significant impact to mental health outcomes, such as self-esteem, anxiety, and depression.[34] Not surprisingly, lower levels of job satisfaction have been shown to be positively related to burnout, a concept we will return to in chapter 5.[35] Who and why some populations tend to experience more or less job satisfaction than others does not always follow logic. For example, the Paradox of the Contented Female Worker describes the observation that women tend to express higher levels of job satisfaction compared to men despite a persistent gender wage gap and disparate rewards.[36] As recently as 2021, women still earned 83 cents to the dollar compared to men in the United States, a difference that's even wider for certain racial groups.[37] Also, job satisfaction tends to increase with age but decline with length of time in any individual job.[38] In other words, the growth in job satisfaction as you age past your thirty-something trough is enjoyed only when you move from job to job and not when you stay in place for your career.

Much of the evidence linking salary to job satisfaction emphasizes the importance of relative over absolute comparisons in predicting worker satisfaction.[39] Income comparisons within the workplace are reportedly more important to happiness than comparing your own affluence to that of your neighbors,[40] an effect that appears stronger for men than women.[41] Employees who identify their salaries as unfair report significantly lower happiness, job, and life satisfaction and are more likely to quit their jobs in the future.[42] David Card and coauthors provide an interesting experimental example of the power of comparisons in their 2012 study looking at the impact of public salary disclosure in the University of California system.[43] University employees who realized under the public disclosure that they ranked below the median salary of comparative colleagues in their fields reported lower job and life satisfaction, and they were more likely to express interest in changing jobs than employees above the median. The alternative of realizing you were above the median pay had no measurable positive impact on reported job satisfaction.

How you view yourself and the world around you may also be an important predictor of job satisfaction. Recent work by Justin Berg and colleagues suggests that workers with a "dual growth mindset," those who view both themselves and their work environment as improvable and changeable, were more likely to implement positive change in their work lives and reported higher levels of sustained happiness compared to workers without a growth mindset or those focused exclusively on changing only the self or the work environment.[44] As it relates to happiness at work, seeing the potential for growth and adaptation in both yourself and the work you do appears to be important predictors of job satisfaction.

SUMMARY

The present chapter paints a nuanced picture of the underlying roots of human happiness and how money and jobs impact health and well-being. First off, happy, positive people tend to live longer and healthier lives. Just ask the nuns! Both economic theory and the data show that money does indeed buy us some happiness but only up to a certain point. The impact of money on our day-to-day moods in the United States appears to cap out at an annual income of about $100,000, although recent debate has shed doubt on the uniformity of that threshold across the happiness spectrum. The data does not show a similar plateau point of money on life satisfaction in the United States, a less mercurial expression of happiness. Globally, the trends are similar, although important regional differences underlying what makes people happy do reveal themselves in the data. For example, money is less important in regions of the world where social connections, family, and friendships take precedence over the power and lure of money.

Happiness appears to be driven largely by relative comparisons as opposed to absolute income. For example, the relationship between money and happiness pivots on how we rank ourselves against our neighbors and colleagues, not in absolute terms. The Easterlin Paradox describes this relationship using data—people with more money are happier, but increases in aggregate wealth do not bring about increases in aggregate happiness on a larger scale. Even as the United States has gotten richer and richer in terms of overall gross domestic product, average happiness has remained stagnant. Some have described this stagnation as a hedonic treadmill, where relative comparisons to our neighbors have us running in place just to keep up with the Joneses.

Job satisfaction, a subset of happiness tied to the work experience, is certainly related to money but is also driven by important nonwage factors, like personality, age, and education. Job satisfaction tends to ebb and flow during a lifetime, with the trough hitting the average worker in their early thirties. Women tend to be more satisfied with their jobs than men despite the gender wage gap, and satisfaction increases with age but not with job tenure. The evidence suggests that much of the growth in satisfaction over a worker's life span is attributed to the forward momentum gained from switching jobs, not from remaining loyal to a single employer. Satisfaction also appears to fluctuate on a shorter time horizon, that is, the Monday blues, and tends to be higher in small versus larger organizations. The salary you make compared to your peers is more important than your actual salary, mirroring trends observed in the overall relationship between money and happiness and the hedonic treadmill.

RECESSIONS, EMPLOYMENT TRENDS, AND WORKER WELL-BEING

It's a recession when your neighbor loses his job; it's a depression when you lose yours.
—President Harry S. Truman

ON THE BRIGHT SIDE

No question about it, Alice Vieira was a hard worker. A product of Depression-era immigrant parents, she was barely a teenager in 1935 when she quit school to work in a candy factory in her hometown of Cambridge, Massachusetts. Figure 3.1 shows Alice with her fellow candy factory workers in the late 1930s. Her father had just passed away from cirrhosis of the liver at age fifty-four, a full-time factory worker who operated a lucrative side business as a bootlegger during Prohibition. Since her mother didn't speak English well, breadwinning responsibilities quickly landed on young Alice's shoulders, and she stepped up like she would do countless more times in her life. She is described by those who knew her as a passionate and intelligent woman; however, a lack of formal education and her gender restricted Alice's prospects for upward mobility in her working life. Fortunately for Alice, factory work in the Boston area was plentiful during much of the twentieth century.

In the 1950s, Alice transitioned from working at the candy factory to the local BF Goodrich factory manufacturing firemen's boots. Hardworking and loyal, she devoted the next two decades of her life to BF Goodrich. During those years, Alice met her husband Joe and gave birth to her only child, Maria. In 1962, Alice and Joe saved enough money to purchase a home in Somerville, Massachusetts, one that remains in the family to this day. The 1950s and 1960s blue-collar lifestyle was predictably good for Alice and her family. It was the calm before the storm.

Figure 3.1
Alice Vieira (bottom right) with fellow workers at the candy factory circa 1939.

Just as Alice was preparing to ring in the 1970s with hope for continued middle-class prosperity, her working world collapsed. Word had been
out for some time that New England factories were abandoning their local
roots for cheaper labor down South. And so it was that about two weeks
before Christmas in 1969, BF Goodrich announced they were relocating
to warmer pastures. For the first time in her adult life, Alice was unemployed. This was a double whammy for Alice, who earlier that year was
diagnosed with breast cancer and was undergoing treatment at the time
of the announcement. Since she and Joe worked at the same factory, there
was no safety net of a second income to float the family finances until Alice
secured another job.

Her daughter Maria, only fourteen at the time, still remembers the
impact of unexpected unemployment on her home life. No doubt this was
a household under intense pressure, and the atmosphere was thick with
stress. Although Alice was eligible for unemployment, hard worker that
she was, she quickly began taking odd jobs to support the family like holi-
day gift wrapping at the local department store. Despite decades of experience in factory work, her search for full-time employment was complicated

Figure 3.2
Alice Vieira inspecting film at Polaroid circa 1972.

by shrinking opportunities in the local manufacturing sector. More and more factories were leaving the Northeast for cheaper labor in other parts of the country.

After two years of searching, struggling, and working odd low-paying jobs to get by, Alice and Joe hit gold when they were both offered employment at the local Polaroid factory. Alice would spend the final decade of her working life in that factory, not missing a single day of work. Her daughter Maria remembers that final phase of her mother's work life at Polaroid as particularly fulfilling for Alice. She enjoyed the work, which was much less physically demanding than her previous BF Goodrich job, and she developed strong relationships with her new colleagues and bosses. Figure 3.2 shows Alice actively engaged in her work tasks at Polaroid.

Alice was described by those who knew her as someone who exuded positivity. She was a genuine human being who was compassionate and generous with family and friends. Drawing upon a famous quote from the Dalai Lama, kindness was her religion. Her daughter Maria describes her mother as someone who never seemed to run out of ways to show that she cared about her. Ultimately, after a tumultuous time of uncertainty, she ended up just where she needed to be. Maria remembers the large family exhale that accompanied the transition to Polaroid, how the house went from an atmosphere of stress to one of job and life satisfaction. Despite the ups and downs of the two previous years, the death of one job opened up the opportunity for something better. Alice eventually retired after fifty years of factory work at the age of sixty-three. Although Joe passed away in 1990, Alice lived another thirty-one years beyond retirement, eventually succumbing to Alzheimer's disease in 2012 at the age of ninety-two.

Alice Vieira's story serves to illustrate how flowers are often born out of the dark soil of an economic downturn. After two decades of hard physical labor at one factory, the rug was pulled out from under her like it was for so many other local factory workers of the era. This put a major strain on her family finances and a few years without Christmas presents under the tree, a penny-pinching experience that brought the family closer together in a common goal. In the end, Alice found a new job and work life that was more satisfying than the last, less physically demanding, and one in which she was ultimately happier up until her retirement a decade later. Alice's health was better served by leaving behind the physically demanding work that she would have otherwise continued for another decade had it not been for that stint of unemployment.

RECESSIONS AND HEALTH

I first became interested in how changes in the economy impact human health while working on a seemingly unrelated topic—diesel exhaust and lung cancer in truck drivers. I started this research at Harvard as part of the appropriately named study TrIPS, or Trucking Industry Particle Study. At that time, the evidence linking air pollution with diseases like lung cancer was still considered by many to be inconclusive. It was not until 2012 that the International Agency for Research on Cancer definitively linked diesel exhaust with lung cancer by identifying it as a known human carcinogen.[1]

As a postdoctoral research fellow, I was given the daunting task of developing a diesel exposure profile for thousands of truckers to match with lung cancer outcomes and determine whether diesel might have contributed to their deaths. While we had substantial amounts of data and detailed information on diesel exposure in the recent past, there was very little to go on for the vast majority of these truckers' work histories, many of whom had decades of experience and exposure on the job. So I went searching for variables that might be related to air pollution to help reconstruct past trends on how much dirty air these workers might have been exposed to on the job. As a newly minted economist, I naturally turned to economic data, looking to employment trends in the trucking industry and economy-wide indicators of the business cycle for clues.

I was surprised to learn when I first started digging that economics had a lot to say about the relationship between a bad economy and human health. The most recent cascade of studies began in 2000 when economist Christopher Ruhm published a paper examining the link between mortality, unemployment, and income across US states.[2] Using more advanced statistical methods than previous studies, Ruhm found strong evidence to support the counterintuitive idea that health actually improves during economic downturns in the form of lower death rates, with the notable exception of deaths by suicide. He argued at the time that reduced employment and income factor into our ability to consume "bads," products like alcohol, cigarettes, and excess food. Also, physical activity might increase as people walk more to avoid the cost of gasoline and vehicle upkeep or eat less food (or eat out less often), decreasing obesity rates. As the story goes, the upside of a down economy is that you have less money to do bad things!

Although much of the subsequent research on economic downturns and population health from across the globe corroborated Ruhm's original findings, other economists have reached the opposite conclusion. Study results vary based on how the data is aggregated (individuals versus county, state or similar geographic level).[3] There are also conflicting results depending on the health outcomes observed, including various measures of chronic health and disability compared to the overall mortality rates observed by Ruhm.[4] Some have suggested that the relationship between economic downturns and health has weakened over time and is no longer as relevant as it was in the past.[5] Depending on the circumstances of the particular recession observed, which industries and workers were hurt most, safety net measures in place, and so on, there are ultimately winners and losers in the health outcomes game.

A growing literature around "deaths of despair," which refer to deaths from drug and alcohol abuse as well as suicides, is drawing attention to the stark reversal of health fortunes among middle-age non-Hispanic White populations in the United States. In one study, researchers estimate that half a million deaths between 1999 and 2013 among middle-age White

Americans could have been avoided had the mortality rate held constant at its 1998 level.[6] A striking rise in drug overdoses, suicides, and chronic liver conditions related to drug and alcohol abuse represent the lion's share of the mortality increases; however, this cohort's lower life expectancy is not mirrored in any other US demographic, age, or ethnicity. Put a bit differently, a White non-Hispanic American between the ages of forty-five and fifty-four today can expect to live a shorter life than their parents.

The steady year-to-year increase in the mortality rate for this age group over more than two decades makes it difficult to attribute deaths of despair to any one specific recession, economic crisis, or labor market trend. Research highlights the potential roots of mortality in the opioid epidemic, accessibility of prescription painkillers, and addiction as well as the physical, mental, and emotional health fallout related to pain, substance abuse, and disability.[7] But an important clue linking these deaths back to the job market is the role of education as a risk factor—90 percent of overdoses in the United States occur in people without a college degree. This group is also more likely to experience "serious mental distress" compared to their more educated peers. Further tying deaths of despair to the workplace, a recent report on Massachusetts workers identified physically demanding blue-collar work as a risk factor in opioid deaths as well as low-paying work, high job insecurity, and lack of paid sick leave.[8]

As the labor market continues its transition toward a technologically advanced and sophisticated service sector, those without a college degree are left with a shrinking share of the pie. Evidence from the sociology literature has related the increase in deaths of despair and particularly drug overdose deaths with de-unionization efforts at the state level.[9] Inequality in work conditions has been referenced by some as a driving force behind growing health inequities nationwide.[10] Interestingly, the precarity and economic insecurity associated with less-skilled work has been associated with increased physical pain, reduced pain tolerance, and a greater use of pain medication, all of which are important risk factors in opioid drug overdoses.[11] And it turns out that it is not only one's own job insecurity but also those of your colleagues and peers that can impact stress and stress-related health outcomes. A study of manufacturing workers during the Great Recession showed that work stress was elevated for remaining workers in downsized plants compared to workers at plants without a high number of layoffs.[12]

Despite the sometimes conflicting evidence presented by dueling economists on the recessions and health dynamic, one thing seems clear: certain groups of people at certain times in history have been better off during recessions. Unemployment is not always a bad thing. No matter how you view it, there is sufficient evidence in the economics literature to justify digging further into the question of what is going on that might improve population health during periods of high unemployment and a bad economy.

My early research on business cycles and air pollution provided an alternative explanation for improvements to health during economic downturns: when there is less economic activity, there is less air pollution. My work identified that both trucking employment and overall unemployment trends tracked with air pollution at the county level in New Jersey and California, the two states with sufficient historical air pollution data to observe these long-term trends. In California, the size of the unemployment swings observed there during the 1980s and 1990s impacted air pollution concentrations on the order of 10–20 percent over that same period.[13] Similar results were observed for New Jersey, where an available marker of diesel pollution (coefficient of haze or COH) tracked closely with economic indicators between 1970 and the mid-1990s. This relationship was particularly noticeable during the major recessionary periods noted in figure 3.3, where peaks in unemployment were matched with troughs in air pollution.[14]

Reduced exposure to air and other sources of pollution that peak during a roaring economy and wane during a weak one might explain some part of the puzzle of healthier populations during recessions and weaker job markets, but it is certainly not the whole picture. As noted earlier, economists have pointed to a few potential factors, most relying on behavior change and reduced consumption of things that are bad for you like cigarettes and alcohol.[15] The unemployed may also have more time for activities like recreational exercise that are squeezed out by tight work schedules.[16] Of course, there is a counter argument to all of this. Studies also show that stress levels are up during recessions and mental health suffers,[17] and drug and alcohol abuse may rise even when alcohol consumption itself is, on average, down.[18] When there is less money for cigarettes and alcohol, there may also be less money to spend on healthy foods.[19] Depending on the scope, scale, and target industries of any given recession, population health outcomes are likely to vary by the individual, industry, and location.

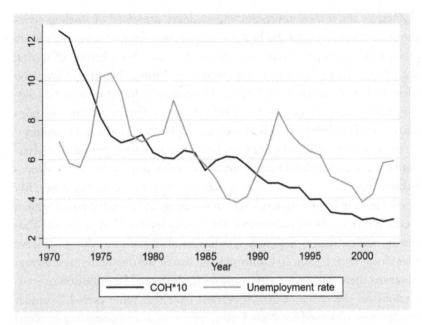

Figure 3.3
Air pollution and unemployment trends in New Jersey, 1970–2000. *Source:* Mary E.
Davis, Francine Laden, Jaime E. Hart, Eric Garshick, and Thomas J. Smith,
"Economic Activity and Trends in Ambient Air Pollution," *Environmental Health
Perspectives* 118, no. 5 (2010): 616.

TRACKING EMPLOYMENT WITH WELL-BEING

UNEMPLOYMENT

Employment status, and particularly periods of unemployment, have been
linked with happiness in several studies around the globe. Although unemployment is often associated with lower levels of happiness on average,[20]
many studies have shown that happiness ultimately returns to baseline
and the effects are not long-lasting.[21] Being unemployed may make you
unhappy initially, but it does not have to keep you unhappy. One explanation for the bounce-back in happiness is called "set point theory," whereby
individuals have their own biologically determined happiness baseline to
which they return after experiencing periods of highs or lows.[22]

In addition to the observation that the ill effects of unemployment on
happiness may not be long-lasting, the evidence shows quite a bit of variability in individual response to unemployment. For example, in a study

of German workers, nearly half of the unemployed population studied reported zero reduction in life satisfaction, and only 5 percent experienced a major decline.[23] Unemployment in Finnish workers did not measurably impact happiness levels of workers in that country during periods of high unemployment in the late 1990s,[24] while the economic crises of the Great Recession in Iceland was shown to have a limited impact on happiness.[25] The evidence suggests that some workers are more adaptable and resilient to negative employment change than others, especially when important safety nets are in place as they are in these European country examples.

Relatedly, research shows that people respond more emotionally to the possibility of a loss compared to a gain, even when the average expected outcome is the same. Put a bit differently, people are, on average, risk averse to a loss (scared to lose something that they already have) but are risk seeking when that same loss is framed as a win.[26] In the context of unemployment and happiness, it suggests that people are likely to be emotionally risk averse to the idea of unemployment but risk loving when unemployment is framed as an opportunity to find a better job. With that in mind, differences in adaptability and resilience to periods of unemployment across individuals and populations, and the impact of these periods of vulnerability on happiness, may ultimately be related to how society and those individuals perceive those changes at the time.

In contrast to unemployment or the absence of employment opportunity, underemployment represents part-time workers who would prefer full-time work. Spikes in the involuntarily underemployed can be a menace to the labor market during periods of economic upheaval. The Great Recession and the more recent COVID shutdown provide stark examples of the vulnerability of workers to both unemployment and underemployment.[27] Research suggests that the drag in chronic underemployment seen in the years after the Great Recession succeeded in keeping US wages from rebounding after the recession.[28]

Emerging research suggests a negative link between involuntary underemployment and worker health and well-being. In a large sample of UK workers, the underemployed (not by choice) reported lower levels of well-being along with rising cases of anxiety and depression; unhappiness grew in proportion to the widening gap between desired hours and actual hours worked.[29] However, it is important to distinguish between workers who are forced into underemployment (above example) versus those who voluntarily choose to work part time. In a recent global study of well-being in older workers using Gallup World Poll data, voluntary part-time workers reported higher levels of happiness and job satisfaction, as well as lower levels of stress and anger, compared to either full-time workers or the involuntarily underemployed.[30]

SELF-EMPLOYMENT

Many workers respond to the call of being their own boss, attracted by the flexibility, autonomy, and control that is often associated with self-employment. But despite the draw that independence holds for some, the percentage of self-employed Americans has gradually declined over the last two decades. However, more recent reports suggest a revival of entrepreneurial spirits in the United States in the wake of the COVID pandemic. As of early 2022, the self-employed represented 11 percent of the US workforce, up from 10 percent in 2015.[31] This uptick in the popularity of self-employment not only reverses a long-term downward slide but also contradicts the usual negative shock to self-employment observed during most recessionary periods.

The historical data suggests that self-employed workers as an aggregate group earn significantly less than wage workers;[32] however, recent evidence disaggregating the self-employed into those running incorporated businesses (entity separate from the worker) versus unincorporated businesses (worker bears sole personal responsibility for the risk) suggests a bimodal earnings distribution.[33] Incorporated self-employment is the most lucrative, while the unincorporated self-employed earn the least of all, with wage earners falling somewhere between those two extremes.

Research points to higher levels of job satisfaction among the self-employed as an aggregate workforce compared to wage workers.[34] With that said, there is a significant amount of heterogeneity among the entrepreneurial classes. Similar to the categories of incorporated versus unincorporated operations, the self-employed can be broken down into two categories based on opportunity and dependency. This distinction between wanting and needing to be self-employed has a drastic impact on the job satisfaction of the self-employed. Opportunity entrepreneurs tend to be more educated and skilled, making an informed choice to move from wage work to self-employment. In contrast, those who respond out of necessity become self-employed due to a lack of options, tend to be less educated and low skilled, and often transition from unemployment to self-employment. This latter group, forced into independence for lack of a better option, tend to experience low employment quality and lower job satisfaction, well-being, and poor health compared to other workers including the opportunistically self-employed who report the highest levels of subjective well-being among the entire workforce.[35]

Moreover, worker demographics and geographic location also factor into how workers derive satisfaction from self-employed activities. For example, one study showed that older self-employed workers were more likely to report having an ideal job than younger ones.[36] In another study, job satisfaction among self-employed UK workers was higher in semiurban locations compared to both urban and rural locations, reflecting important quality of life and location characteristics that enhance the well-being of independent workers.[37]

The self-employed are much less likely to have health insurance compared to wage employees. Nearly one in four self-employed workers in the United States does not have health insurance even after increased access under the Affordable Care Act.[38] Despite this, the self-employed tend to compare favorably on health compared to wage workers, with self-employment positively associated with perceived physical health and healthy lifestyle choices, along with lower rates of chronic illness such as diabetes, high blood pressure, high cholesterol, and arthritis.[39]

UNIONIZATION

For decades, economists have explored the relationship between unionization and worker well-being, focusing initially on its impact on job satisfaction. George Borjas was the first to report a negative correlation between unionism and job satisfaction in a large national cohort of US men.[40] In his seminal 1979 paper, he posited a number of plausible explanations for the negative trends. First off, union members may be more aware of the unpleasant aspects of their jobs, which may drive them toward unionization in the first place. Also, union members experience flatter earnings potential and wage growth compared to those in nonunionized workplaces. With that in mind, it is not surprising that Borjas observed a stronger negative relationship on job satisfaction for workers with more tenure on the job since these workers were more likely to have come up against stunted wage growth.

Although a significant amount of research over the last few decades have generally supported Borjas's conclusions, recent studies have begun to pick apart at the generally accepted norm that job satisfaction is lower among union members. Using more advanced statistical techniques that control for reverse causality, a recent study observed a positive effect of unions on job satisfaction, although the impact was not long-lasting.[41] Additional evidence suggests that the negative relationship observed by Borjas may no longer be relevant in the post-2000 economy as more recent birth cohorts experience the benefits of unionization differently than their predecessors.[42]

Although unionization has been linked indirectly with various positive aspects of the worker health experience like access to health insurance, improved workplace conditions, and reduced income inequality,[43] there is no reliable evidence in the economics literature tying unions directly with improved overall health.[44] In fact, research points to a negligible effect, at best, of union membership on reducing incidences of poor worker health outcomes, including mental health.[45] Despite a historically strong advocacy role around workplace safety, some have suggested that unions are behind the curve on addressing modern-day work hazards related to psychosocial stressors, work-life balance, and burnout.[46]

According to the most recent data from the BLS, unions lost 241,000 members in 2021 compared to 2020, a continuation of a long-term downward trend in the United States.[47] Current union membership is about half what it was in 1983, with the largest decline over time coming from membership losses in the private sector.[48] Recent accounts of unionization among certain sectors and high-profile businesses like Starbucks and Amazon provide some newsworthy fodder for a potential shift in union fortunes; even with the current decline, some job categories and geographies have seen recent union gains despite aggregate losses. One signal that the tides may be turning against the long-term slide is the recent uptick in the union representation petitions received by the National Labor Relations Board, which have increased more than 50 percent in 2021 compared to 2020.[49] Interest is on the rise even as participation is declining. It remains to be seen whether unions will make a sustained comeback in the post-COVID economy.

AND THEN THERE WAS COVID

The COVID epidemic has brought with it economic upheaval and a massive spike in unemployment not seen since the Great Depression era nearly one hundred years ago. Not surprisingly, air pollution levels dropped to unprecedented lows as global economic and transport activity slowed to a crawl.[50] Unemployment levels in 2020 dwarfed all modern-day crises and business cycles over the last thirty years, including the oil crises of the 1970s, harsh recessions of the 1980s and 1990s, and the more recent Great Recession and housing and financial crises. But that unemployment tide rolled out as quickly as it rolled in, swiftly followed by record-low unemployment in 2022. Disentangling the effects of unprecedented unemployment swings from the impact of COVID itself on general health outcomes, longevity, and happiness will take some time to fully understand the long-term consequences.

Despite uncertainties around how the pandemic will ultimately impact the topics covered in this chapter, unprecedented levels of job shifting, resignations, retirements, and temporary absences from the labor force suggest a paradigm shift in how workers relate to their jobs. More than a quarter of US workers are expected to transition to new occupations by 2030 as a result of the post-COVID labor market shift from low- to high-wage sectors. According to a research report by McKinsey Global Institute,[51] these new jobs will require many workers to retrain and develop more technical and socioemotional skills than their previous jobs that relied on physicality and basic cognitive skills. Women, those without college education, young, and minority workers will be disproportionately impacted by this labor market transition since they are overrepresented in the low-tier service jobs that are expected to contract.

Interestingly, the most upheaval in the labor market appears to be occurring in the population demographic approaching middle age (thirty to forty-five), with a 20 percent bump in resignations over the single year between 2020 and 2021.[52] As a worker at the top of this age group, I draw from my own experiences to understand why I might be at higher "resignation risk" than someone at the beginning or end of their careers. First off, I am staring down the "middle" of my work life, half of it behind me and half of it left to go. At this middle point, I have a perspective of the past and an expectation for the future, a duality that neither new workers nor retirement-age workers possess. And according to the happiness literature, middle age corresponds to the least happy period of my lifespan. If a paradigm shift is indeed what is on the horizon, it is not surprising that workers in the midsection of their work lives with the perspective, desire, and ability to change their work circumstances are the ones driving it. Workers appear emboldened to change their expectations for work and how it contributes to their overall quality of life.

SUMMARY

This chapter explores the role of recessions and employment on worker health and well-being. Much of the evidence points to a counterintuitive positive effect of recessions on health. Historically, people tend to be healthier in bad economic times. The health boost has been attributed to a more active lifestyle and less money to engage in health-limiting consumption as well as lowered exposure to the pollution generated by economic activity. The exception to positive health during recessions are deaths of despair, or those attributed to suicide, drug, and alcohol abuse. An alarming increase in deaths of despair outside of the business cycle has been observed over the last twenty years, particularly among White low-skilled workers without a college degree.

Evidence suggests a worker's brush with unemployment does lower well-being in the short run but that the effects do not appear to be long-lasting. Underemployment manifests in a range of negative health and well-being effects unless it is a conscious choice on the part of the worker. The relationship between self-employment and health and well-being depends on the worker's skill and education level and whether they are considered opportunity versus necessity entrepreneurs. High-skilled workers who choose self-employment rank as the most satisfied in the workforce, while those who are self-employed for lack of a better option are the least satisfied. Wage workers lie somewhere between these two self-employment satisfaction extremes. Similar to previous descriptions of gig work and platform dependency, choice is the most important indicator of health and well-being in relation to a worker's experience with periods of unemployment, underemployment, and self-employment.

Although unionization has experienced a steady decline in the United States over the last fifty years, recent increases in petitions for union representation may signal a change in fortunes for unions in the post-COVID economy. Historically, the relationship between unionization and job satisfaction has been observed to be negative. There is no doubt that unions provide important health-promoting benefits to workers, but the evidence is spotty on whether those benefits translate into better health outcomes in the unionized workforce. It is possible that unionized workers are less satisfied with their work because they are more aware of the negative aspects of the job, or over time experience more constrained wage growth as a result of wage compression. Recent research provides evidence that the negative well-being effects of unionization may not be representative of modern-day worker experiences, who reflect on the benefits of unionization differently than their predecessors.

The impact of COVID on the employment landscape in the United States cannot be overstated. Wide swings in unemployment and job shifting have rocked the job market over just a few short years. The biggest group of job shifters appear to be middle-agers, the most unhappy demographic of the lifespan. One in four workers are predicted to shift not just jobs but all new occupations over the next ten years, following a wave of contraction in the low-skilled labor market. It is challenging to anticipate the settling point for all of this labor market chaos, but it may be far from over.

4

MEANINGFUL WORK

> Life is never made unbearable by circumstances, but only by lack of meaning
> and purpose.
> —Viktor Frankl

A PITSTOP TO SOMETHING BETTER

I started working part-time jobs as soon as I had a license to drive. Over
that next decade while pursuing my education, I worked my way through
more part-time jobs than I can count on my fingers and toes. I can barely
remember all the faces and situations so many years later, with the exception of my very first work experience the summer before my junior year of
high school. Quite possibly the dirtiest job I have ever done, I worked that
summer and another four or so after that at a convenience store on the side
of a state highway in rural central Florida. Besides running the register sell-
ing snacks and gas, cigarettes and 40s, I also mopped floors, cleaned toilets,
cashed out the rare winning lottery ticket, stocked the beer, and kept the
gas pumps flowing. But in truth, the dirty tasks and physicality of the job
are not what stand out in my mind all these years later. We all have to start
somewhere, and what better place to start my own work journey than off
of the side of a dusty, dirty highway?

Hard work was, of course, a lesson in and of itself, a motivation of sorts
to do well in school and expand my work life opportunities beyond mop-
ping floors. My earliest employment taught me the value of hard work as
a means to an end. But the far more valuable lesson that I took away from
that experience was not the value of hard work per se but the value of the
people who do the hard work. My first supervisor on that first job was a
woman named Darlene. Darlene was the real deal. She had fiery red curly
hair that she wore in a classic Southern mullet style (short on top, long in

the back) and spoke with a bold Southern drawl that left no doubt of her roots. She had graduated just a few years before me from the local high school and had quickly risen from cashier to manager in record time.

Despite my book smarts, it quickly became clear as Darlene took charge of training me that I had a lot to learn. I lacked intuition for real-world work. It was Darlene's task to guide me, to train me not only in the operation and maintenance of the store but in how to work *well*. She was efficient, an excellent problem solver, a clear communicator, and a fair manager. Not surprisingly, our store was one of the best performing and well-maintained of all the affiliated chain of convenience stores. That was in no small part due to Darlene's work ethic.

What I remember most about Darlene was her approach to work. Managing a gas station was not glamorous by any measure, but she worked with a sense of pride in her job. Despite the perceived lowliness of the tasks, Darlene was purposeful in her approach and connected to the job in a way that stood out in comparison to the other employees and managers I observed in the convenience stores over that time. I could imagine Darlene running an ER ward at the hospital saving lives with the same passion and zeal for her work that I observed her running a lowly gas station in rural America.

Despite her connectedness to her work in the moment, Darlene was not without higher aspirations. She managed to save enough money over time from the low-wage work to return to school to become an accountant, a job that would be less physically demanding and more financially rewarding than retail management. Darlene was not blind to the inequities. The convenience store was not her destination. But she was capable of leveraging every moment of her time in that dirty job as important. Darlene taught me it was possible to derive pride from any work, not just work considered desirable by society.

MEANINGFUL LIFE

Chapter 2 outlined three aspects of subjective well-being that illustrate how the academic research defines happiness—affective, evaluative, and eudaemonic well-being. To summarize, affective well-being ebbs and flows with mood and situation, fluctuating based on day-to-day experiences and challenges. Researchers attempting to capture affective well-being ask questions about the presence and frequency of various emotional states, both good and bad, that someone has experienced recently or over a specific time period. In contrast, evaluative well-being represents a more durable relationship with contentedness in life and is often identified by questions about how satisfied individuals are with their lives overall. Although day-to-day mood and overall life satisfaction are, on many levels, related to each other, they do not necessarily go hand in hand. Someone could be very satisfied with their lives overall but miserable in the day-to-day situations and vice versa.

Human experiences and states of being, like wealth, employment, health, and longevity relate differently to affective and evaluative well-being. For example, the level of income needed to report happiness in the day-to-day experience is significantly lower than what is required to report high levels of life satisfaction. Put a bit differently, short-term well-being is easier to manipulate with money than long-term happiness.

The third measure of subjective well-being, known as eudaemonic well-being, is defined as a sense of meaning or purpose in life. The concept of eudaemonic well-being has roots in ancient Greek philosophy, described by Aristotle in *Nicomachean Ethics* as the condition of "living well or doing well."[1] Happiness, Aristotle notes, "is the highest of all practical goods." What distinguishes eudaemonic well-being from the two other forms of subjective well-being is that it is neither a feeling nor a perception; instead, it represents the sustained pursuit of something greater than oneself. It encompasses a commitment to personal growth, acceptance of both circumstances and self, and a sense of autonomy. Compared to the other two measures of well-being, eudaemonic involves a degree of introspection that accumulates over time and involves more complex thought than either current mood or life satisfaction.[2]

Twentieth-century psychologist Viktor Frankl reinvigorated the modern-day discussion of eudaemonic well-being in his autobiography recounting his survival in World War II Nazi concentration camps. From Frankl's perspective, eudaemonic well-being is a goal of human existence that transcends even the most horrific circumstances and life stressors. He wrote, "The way in which a man accepts his fate and all the suffering it entails, the way in which he takes up his cross, gives him ample opportunity—even under the most difficult circumstances—to add a deeper meaning to his life."[3]

Not surprisingly, higher levels of eudaemonic well-being have been associated with a range of positive human health benefits. In a study of

Chicago seniors, those who described themselves with more purpose and meaning had a lower risk of Alzheimer's disease,[4] were more mobile and independent, and had a lower risk of becoming disabled.[5] In a national survey of older US adults, purpose and meaning were linked to reduced risk of stroke[6] and stronger functional activity measures such as hand grip strength and walking speed.[7] Additionally, greater purpose has been associated with reduced risk of arthritis in a cohort of European seniors.[8] More generally, eudaemonic well-being represents an important factor predicting longevity and improved quality of life.[9]

Frankl surmised that people with a greater sense of purpose and meaning live longer because they have a stronger will to live. More recent evidence in support of his hypothesis suggests that people with higher purpose are more proactive about their health. In a representative sample of US adults over the age of fifty, higher purpose was associated with an increased use of preventative health services and reduced hospital stays.[10]

DEFINING MEANINGFUL WORK

The definition of meaningful work varies across studies, albeit in a similar thread. It is described in raw terms as a net positive work experience that enhances physical, cognitive, and emotional energy in return for work deemed valuable and worthwhile.[11] Taking a more nuanced view of meaningful work, it can be defined as a multifaceted sensation of eudaemonic well-being made up of a positive relationship with work, interconnectedness between work and personal life, and a contribution of work toward the greater good.[12]

Frankl identified work as one of the ways that humans can discover meaning in his recounting of life in concentration camps. He observed among his fellow inmates that meaningful work served as a defense against physical and mental breakdown. He shared a story of his own experience with meaningful work while suffering and nearly dying from typhoid fever. During that dark time, his only attachment to life was the simple act of making notes on scraps of paper so that he could eventually reconstruct the manuscript taken from him upon his internment. The desire to ultimately complete and publish his life's work sustained his will to live and, quite literally, saved his life.

Extending the concept of meaningful work to the well-known Maslow's hierarchy of needs,[13] meaningful work engenders an authentic connection between the work and nonwork parts of life in a way that can open the gates of higher purpose, to appreciate and understand our place in the world. Within Maslow's framework, meaningful work is a key ingredient in striving toward self-transcendence, the apex of Maslow's pyramid and the highest achievement and manifestation of well-being.

THE CASE OF NUNS

When it comes to occupations closely associated with meaningful work, I naturally think of those engaged in work dedicated to a higher power or God. Chapter 2 described one such group of workers—twentieth-century US Catholic nuns. A narrow view of women religious in America might erroneously pigeonhole these sisters into a work life spent cloistered in silence and prayer. That solitary and singular existence is favored by so-called contemplative nuns, whose primary vocation is in fact prayer. Contemplative nuns devote their daily lives to prayer for the world and its people and as such do not work outside the convent and are rarely seen in public. Their life is punctuated only by purposeful work and group service to maintain the cloistered community life and, yes, lots of prayer.

But these contemplative nuns are less the rule than the exception. Especially for those nuns born during the early 1900s whose writing style, sentiments, health and longevity were observed as part of the Nun Study of Aging and Alzheimer's Disease,[14] working outside the convent walls in the service of God was a nonnegotiable part of the nun's job description. In fact, the first nuns to arrive in America were explicitly recruited and contracted to fill key service professions in the New World. That first cohort of Ursuline sisters arrived in the French colonial city of New Orleans in 1727 and immediately went to work as teachers and nurses.[15]

In many respects, nuns represent early America's first essential workforce, providing cheap labor to fill critical service roles in teaching, health care, and social services for the growing nation. They were often brought in to care for patients with infectious diseases like cholera, typhoid, and tuberculosis when lay nurses refused to take the personal risk. They helped staff field hospitals during the many wars in US history, again risking their lives in selfless service to others. Nuns helped establish, lead, and staff the growing number Catholic institutions, including schools, churches, orphanages, and hospitals. In one example, a large donation from Joseph and Rose Kennedy is credited with creating the Franciscan Children's hospital in Boston, which opened in 1949. The hospital would not have been possible without the Franciscan Sisters of Mary, forty of whom lived and served at the hospital during the early years.[16] Although their male counterparts are often given credit for the rapid growth in Catholic institutions over US history, in terms of aggregate labor contribution, nuns outnumbered priests by four to one in most urban parishes.[17]

Nuns enjoyed a unique degree of work autonomy at a time when the vast majority of women in America were excluded from the paid labor force. Many nuns received an advanced education to support the highest levels of service within their professions. For example, communities of women-religious-sponsored nursing schools trained both Catholics and laywomen to enter the health-care profession. By 1968, nuns comprised half of the faculty and administrator positions at the 142 Catholic women's colleges in existence.[18] During that time, nearly every department within the US Catholic hospital system was administratively led by a nun. At a time of limited opportunities for laywomen, Catholic nuns were making their way to the top of critical service organizations before the glass ceiling was even a thing.

It is interesting to consider the stark differences in life expectancy between laywomen born at the beginning of the 1900s versus their peers who chose the sisterhood. A US woman born in 1917 could expect to live an average of fifty-four years.[19] By comparison, women of that same generation who elected a life of service to God at age twenty eventually lived thirty-plus years longer, on average. The Nun Study attributed the variability in longevity within the sampled nuns to differences in personality and positive affect, which provided a statistically significant boost in life expectancy of around seven years.[20] However, the biggest longevity boost came from simply choosing the work life of a nun, on the order of thirty-two to forty years of extra life depending on the nun's positivity ranking. It is difficult to know the extent to which a fulfilling and meaningful work life contributed to the years of life gained over their lay counterparts. A myriad of other factors in their environments and biology also contributed to these differences, such as mortality risk factors related to childbirth. But the fact that nuns had access to meaningful work experiences by virtue of their presence in the labor force sets them apart from other women of their

generations. Taken in the context of the academic literature linking meaningful work with longevity, health, and well-being, it provides a plausible
explanation for the differences in health outcomes across the two groups.

The early monumental progress in the work lives of nuns as social service
pioneers over much of US history was met with an equally steep decline in
the nun labor force participation rate during the second half of the twentieth century. Although the occupations of priests and nuns have both been
declining over the last fifty years, the drop off in nuns is the most striking of
the two groups. According to data from the Center for Applied Research in
the Apostolate, the number of US nuns dropped 80 percent between 1970
and 2020, compared to a 42 percent decline among US priests.[21] While the
trend in priests is consistent with the overall downward trajectory in male
labor force participation over that same time period, the declining participation of nuns is in stark contrast to the steady increase in women's participation in the US workforce over the last half century (figure 4.1). During

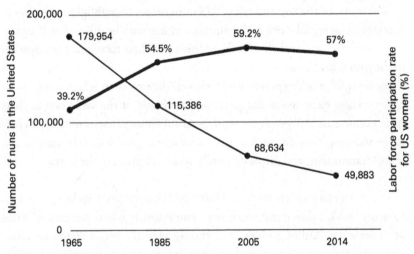

Figure 4.1
Nuns and female labor force participation in the United States, 1965 to 2014. *Source:*
Michael Lipka, "US Nuns Face Shrinking Numbers and Tensions with the Vatican,"
Pew Research Center, August 8, 2014, https://www.pewresearch.org/fact-tank/2014
/08/08/u-s-nuns-face-shrinking-numbers-and-tensions-with-the-vatican/; Federal
Reserve Bank of St. Louis, "Women in the Labor Force," *The FRED Blog*, March 8,
2021. https://fredblog.stlouisfed.org/2021/03/women-in-the-labor-force/.

Note: The left axis and lighter shaded line represent the total number of nuns in the United States; the
right axis and the darker shaded line represent the labor force participation rate for US women overall.

that time, compensated work outside the home became the norm instead of the exception, bringing women closer to parity with men in access to meaningful work.

The impact of the decline in nuns has been felt deeply across Catholic social service institutions. The number of nuns and priests working in parochial schools dropped 50 percent between 1975 and 1989. Declining access to the nuns' cheap yet skilled labor placed a burden on parochial schools to hire lay teachers who demanded higher salaries, ultimately increasing labor costs so much that many long-standing schools were forced to close or merge to cut costs. Catholic hospitals have also felt the pinch. The number of nun nurses declined 35 percent in the decade between 1965 and 1975. By 2011, there were only eleven nuns reportedly employed by the largest network of Catholic hospitals in the United States, and none of them were administrators.[22] Not surprisingly, the loss of cheap skilled labor was a major financial hit on Catholic hospitals, and like their parochial school counterparts, many were forced to merge or close.

The story of the rise and fall of US nuns serves to highlight inequities in access to meaningful work and their relationship with health and well-being. Expanded occupational choices for women and their increased participation in the paid workforce over time has helped to level the playing field in access to meaningful work experiences. However, the extent to which women can capture these experiences for personal fulfillment at the same rate as their male counterparts depends on many societal factors that continue to challenge working women, such as pay imbalances, gender discrimination and sexual harassment, and disparate family responsibilities in the home.

INTERDISCIPLINARY STUDY OF MEANINGFUL WORK

In many ways, meaningful work is a "you know it when you feel it" kind of experience. Although we can certainly identify broad trends or characteristics that on average tend to promote or impede meaningful work, its presence or absence is ultimately unique to the person, place, and time. What brings meaning to one individual or group may not provide a similar sense of purpose to another individual or group. Meaningful work for one generation may not be experienced equally in subsequent generations. Even within an individual's lifespan, meaningful work will adapt and change throughout the various stages of development, from a young working adult through retirement and old age.

My brief stint as a drug cop provided early insight into the highly individualized experience of meaningful work. The ultimate purpose of my
job was to stop illegal drugs from entering the United States during the
height of the War on Drugs. Many of my fellow recruits were ex-military
and embarking upon a second career in law enforcement. In contrast, I
was a freshly minted college graduate with a degree in economics. They
possessed a strong sense of "honor" and duty and derived meaning from
continued service to their country. I shared neither their life experiences
nor their resolve for drug interdiction. I was ambivalent to drugs, neither
a user nor a critic. But I did initially feel that my job contributed to the
greater good by keeping people safe, even if drugs were not high on my
priority list.

But as I came to do my job every day, I grew increasingly unsettled by
the power dynamics. On the US border, officers do not need probable cause
to conduct a search. Mere suspicion, regardless of whether that suspicion
is grounded in stereotype or bias, is sufficient to justify a search, including
intrusive body searches. The vast majority of officers were men, while the
preponderance of travelers stopped and searched on suspicion of smuggling
drugs were women, most of whom were Black or Brown. The unbalanced
gender ratio of the searches was based on a widely held assumption that
women from certain countries in the Caribbean and Latin America represented most drug mules entering Miami at that time. Confused at first
by what I saw, I naively asked my on-the-job trainer why he only stopped
women from certain countries. He returned with a matter of fact response:
"Because they're the ones bringing in the drugs." When I asked him how he
knew that to be true if he only ever stopped this group of women, he just
puffed and assured me that it was a known fact. In another example, one
day I arrived to work and found a Post-it note stuck to my workstation that
had been circulated to all officers on duty that day mandating that we stop
and search all female flight attendants coming from a certain country. The
search directive was based on an anonymous and ambiguous tip received
that morning that an unnamed flight attendant intended to smuggle drugs
that day. No other details were necessary to subject all female flight attendants that likely numbered in the hundreds to intrusive searches.

Although I tried to bring awareness to these issues—for example, I con-
tested the flight attendant note by bringing it directly to the director of
operations—I also found myself in a delicate position of trying to prove

my worth to my male peers. I did my best to flag the major issues while being aware in my own search activity to avoid common biases in practice during that time. But since port policy forbade cross-gender body searches and I was often one of the only female officers nearby, I was regularly brought in to conduct the intrusive parts of female searches or to just be present as a female witness during a search. So despite my resistance toward conducting stereotyped searches, I was involved daily in them. I began to feel more and more dissatisfied with my work role, which felt increasingly misaligned with my core values. On the positive side, I was playing a small part in stopping drugs from hitting the streets of the United States. However, I was arresting low-level smugglers targeted for their race and gender. I came to empathize with their situations in a way that made it difficult to do my job.

But my experience with meaningless work was not universal. In fact, many of my colleagues thrived in their jobs and appeared to derive satisfaction and meaning from the role they played in society. They appeared largely ignorant and unaffected by the impact of gender and racial bias in their enforcement decisions. In short, my experience with the meaninglessness of that particular job was not a shared experience across the majority of my peers doing exactly the same work. So I quit. But the experience was not without its life lessons. Not the least of which, I learned what I did *not* want to do for work.

The scientific study of meaningful work is an eclectic one, peaking the interest of disciplines like occupational health, organizational behavior, psychology, humanities and ethics, and human resources development. Each disciplinary perspective sets its own norms and baselines with respect to the definition and operationalization of meaningful work. An advantage of this broad scientific interest is that it provides multiple vantage points and perspectives and ultimately a more wholistic picture of meaningful work.

A central theme emerges from the meaningful work literature pointing to a highly subjective and individualized experience that is difficult to aggregate into a one-size-fits-all model. Meaningful work is motivated by both internal and external factors that will vary by worker, situation, and timing. Meaningful work is present when the individual worker with unique life experiences, aspirations, and beliefs feels that it is, irrespective of whether the work satisfies some list of meaningful work indicators. It is for this reason that many well-intentioned organizational-level strategies to manufacture meaningful work experiences fail to result in a more engaged and invested workforce. Meaningful work belongs to the worker, not the employer.

Many studies have attempted to operationalize meaningful work and quantitatively or qualitatively measure and assess the experience across workers and settings, as well as its relationship to health and other measures of well-being.[23] Despite these attempts, researchers have found it challenging to distinguish the multifaceted meaningful work experience from more one-dimensional measures like job satisfaction, motivation, and engagement. In one scoring system developed using factor analytic techniques, four primary dimensions of meaningful work were identified, including developing the inner self, unity with others, serving others, and expressing full potential.[24] The second and third factors signal strong interpersonal relationships across the workplace and toward the people or communities serviced by the work. They require a sense of belonging, mutual respect, and commitment to the people around them. The other two factors are intrapersonal in the sense that they represent a personal experience not shared with others. They require freedom to express creativity and talents, a sense of achievement, and the ability to grow toward and become one's true self. Importantly, the realization of meaningful work requires a level of self-awareness and self-knowledge on the part of the worker, who can either be supported or stunted by the work and work environment.

We can imagine these dimensions as a four-seated teeter totter on a child's playground. For this childhood staple to remain in overall balance, all four children must be relatively equal in size and work together. A meaningful work experience evokes a similar tension between the interpersonal commitment to others balanced against the intrapersonal commitment to oneself, as well as the ability to contemplate and reflect balanced against a drive to action. A truly meaningful work experience exists when all four dimensions are emphasized to a similar degree and work together to support a balanced work experience.

A recent meta-analysis of the research on meaningful work explored the gamut of perspectives that have contributed to our understanding of the topic.[25] In their comprehensive review of the existing literature, researchers identified five basic categories that represent important antecedents to the experience of meaningful work. Table 4.1 identifies these categories as job

Table 4.1
Meaningful work

Predictors of meaningful work	Aspects that advance meaningful work	Aspect that oppose meaningful work
Job design	Task significance, variety, clarity, and identity; tasks that are challenging, creative, and autonomous; fit to role	Pointless tasks
Leadership and management	Transformational, spiritual, and supportive leadership; strong and open communication; participatory and constructive management styles	Abusive and divisive leadership or supervision
Organizational	Spiritual, learning-focused environment; self-selected teams; community orientation; access to resources	Absence of these characteristics
Workplace relationships	Positive interpersonal relationships, manager recognition	Absence of positive relationships or presence of negative workplace relationships
Work life	Balance	Conflict

Source: Catherine Bailey, Ruth Yeoman, Adrian Madden, Marc Thompson, and Gary Kerridge, "A Review of the Empirical Literature on Meaningful Work: Progress and Research Agenda," *Human Resource Development Review* 18, no. 1 (2019): 83–113.

design, leadership and management, organizational, workplace relationships, and work life.

Job design factors that promote a worker's experience with meaningfulness include important and variable tasks that require creativity and autonomy and represent a good fit to the worker's skill set. The antithesis of meaningful tasks is work that is perceived as pointless. Leadership and management factors that promote meaningfulness include strong and supportive leaders who engender open and participatory communication styles. The opposite of this are leaders who are abusive or divisive in their supervision of subordinates. In terms of organizational factors, meaningfulness is supported in settings that are spiritual, community focused, and learning centric, where workers can self-select their teams and have access to the resources needed to do their jobs. Workplace relationships that complement meaningfulness are those considered positive, where managers recognize the good work of their employees. Finally, work-life balance is an important element of meaningfulness, while work-life conflict can serve as an impediment.

Related research provides a slightly different take on the makeup of meaningful work, operationalizing four separate domains that include tasks, role, interpersonal interactions, and organization.[26] Tasks reflect factors such as the level of skill required, perceived importance or significance of the tasks, and the degree to which a worker can identify with the tasks they perform. Role goes beyond the definition of task to identify the norms and expectations of the work, including whether it is considered good or bad, or high or low status. Interpersonal interactions represent those relationships that occur both within and outside the organization related to work. And finally, the organization itself provides the baseline environment where meaning and personal growth can be either fostered or stunted.

Very little research is available tracking differences in meaningful work across occupational groups, and none provide any sort of rigorous test of causality. Limited evidence suggests that white-collar workers score higher on most dimensions of meaningful work compared to blue- and pink-collar workers.[27] Pink-collar workers include those jobs in care-oriented fields that have historically been considered women's work, for example, childcare, nursing, social work, and beauty services. However, no fine-grained studies are available beyond the crude aggregate collar-level groupings that account for important factors such as education level and financial reward. With that in mind, it is challenging to pinpoint any sort of valid occupational differences or to interpret the reasoning for the correlational trends observed across "collar" groupings.

MEANINGFUL VERSUS MEANINGLESS WORK

Can the supportive factors underlying meaningful work be reversed to opposite effect, in other words, to degrade work into meaningless experiences? Some researchers have attempted to disentangle meaningful from meaningless work to determine whether they operate along a continuum (more of one, less of the other) or represent separable concepts.[28] Research on the topic suggests that meaningful work originates as an internal (personal) experience of the worker who is not easily manipulated by external (organization) factors and circumstances. Stated a bit differently, while

Table 4.2

The role of the organization in meaningless work

Personal drivers of meaningful work	Organizational drivers of meaningless work
Self-transcendent: work that brings meaning to both others and self	Disconnect of values between worker and organization
Challenging: one in which difficult situations can be addressed and resolved	Worker taken for granted or not recognized for positive achievements
Episodic and memorable: as opposed to sustained over time	Pointless or bureaucratic work
Reflective: experienced in retrospect with contemplation as opposed to in the moment	Unfair treatment
	Forced to ignore one's better judgment Lack of supportive relationships Unnecessary risk of emotional or physical harm

Source: Catherine Bailey and Adrian Madden, "What Makes Work Meaningful—Or Meaningless," *MIT Sloan Management Review* 57, no. 4 (2016): 53–61.

meaningful work experiences are internal to the individual worker, meaningless work is more likely to be connected to the organization, misaligned organizational values, and poor treatment of workers. Most importantly, workers are more likely to perceive work as meaningless when they work under poorly constructed management practices. Table 4.2 highlights the dichotomy between the personal and organizational factors underlying a worker's experience with meaning.

Meaningful work is personal, epitomized by challenging effort that is important to both self and others and is often experienced in memorable bursts or when reflecting on past experiences. In contrast, meaningless work is organizational, existing in situations where organizational values are poorly aligned or misunderstood; where workers are taken for granted, treated unfairly, or lack supportive relationships from colleagues and managers; where workers are forced to act against their better judgment; or where work is unnecessarily risky.

Also falling under the organization purview for meaningless work are tasks that are perceived as boring, pointless, or overly bureaucratic. When workers are not connecting with meaning and purpose in their work lives, it can manifest as boredom, a kind of existential vacuum for the worker's soul. The resulting disengagement and apathy toward work ultimately leads to disaffected workers, turnover, and burnout.[29] It is hard to overstate the negative impact of pointless and boring tasks on the experience of meaningfulness. Bored and disaffected workers are referred to by some as "existential labor";[30] anthropologist David Graeber popularized this concept as "bullshit jobs," drawing attention to the increasing trend in pointless work as spiritual violence against the modern-day worker.[31]

In a 2022 industry report, "interesting work" ranked highly among top priority job attributes in a survey of international workers. Interesting work was second only to compensation as the most important consideration in taking and keeping a job. A number of other factors related to meaningful work also scored highly for workers, including relationships with coworkers, opportunities for learning and growth, a job that is helpful to society, and an inspiring company.[32]

THE EXPERIENCE OF MEANINGFUL WORK OVER TIME

Meaningful work is an experience that ebbs and flows in even the most purposeful of work-worker connections. It can be experienced in bursts depending on factors both internal and external to the worker or as a sustained relationship of work as a calling.[33] Some workers may identify their job as meaningful only in retrospect, while others may experience that connection in the present moment. Still, others might derive meaning from work as an aspirational goal, something they are striving or working toward as opposed to identifying it as a past or present experience.

As noted above, some workers may choose to pursue a career based on an aspirational goal to find meaningfulness, such as jobs that present an opportunity to serve others like nursing, teaching, and social services. However, it is not guaranteed that once on the job these workers will experience the meaning they desire, particularly under poor organizational practices or work settings where they are undervalued or otherwise unable to express their full potential.

The case of nurses, especially during the pandemic, provide a critical example of this phenomenon. As a caring profession, nurses are more likely than others to be "called" to their occupations with a desire to serve others in need. No doubt, the COVID pandemic put a significant strain on health care and nurses as the frontline workers in patient care. Not surprisingly, in a 2021 survey of nurses conducted during the height of the pandemic, 32 percent reported they were considering leaving direct care with patients, a 10 percent increase over just ten months earlier.[34] Of those nurses who planned to stay in direct patient care, the decision weighed more heavily on job attributes related to meaningful work, positive coworker relationships, and a sense of engagement and belonging. The most important factors in the decision for those frontline nurses considering leaving direct patient care focused on what they perceived to be an unmanageable workload. Overall, nurses who valued meaningful work were more resilient to the myriad of workload stressors and challenges faced by the unprecedented strain on the pandemic-era nurse.

RETIREMENT AND MEANINGFUL WORK

If meaningful work represents an important component of eudaemonic well-being, it begs the question of whether retirement from meaningful work impacts late-life health and longevity. The retirement effects are tricky to uncover because we first need to know whether the work before retirement was considered meaningful to the individual worker. Freedom from meaningless work will impact someone very differently than the abrupt absence of meaningful work. Unfortunately, no studies to date have tracked meaningful work as a modifier of the relationship between retirement and longevity. Beyond the absence of meaningful work measures, the endogeneity and interdependence of the two variables are further confounded by a strong healthy worker effect. In general, healthy people tend to work longer, while people in poorer health tend to retire earlier due to health limitations. Since retirement is to varying degrees a personal choice, embedded within that choice may be many unobserved factors such as bad health, cognitive decline, or worker time preferences.

Beyond the meaningful work connection, the evidence linking retirement with health and longevity is itself mixed. A meta-analysis of longitudinal studies representing the strongest evidence linking retirement with late-life health and longevity found no association between early retirement and mortality but a higher risk of mortality for on-time retirement compared to remaining in the workforce.[35] Additional evidence from a cross-country study of European workers points to improved health among retirees from physically demanding and strenuous work in contrast to the negative effects on aggregate for the full sample of workers.[36] In a global sample of workers from the Gallup World Poll, retirees who voluntarily chose to continue working were happier and experienced lower levels of stress and anger compared to the fully retired.[37] However, the health benefits of late-life employment did not hold for workers who were forced to continue working for financial reasons.

Reflecting back on Bob our fisher, it was clear based on my conversation with him that he considered his work to be quite meaningful. The identities of Bob and many other fishers that I interviewed were so closely intertwined with their work that it would be hard to distinguish meaning and purpose separately from work and their personal lives. Most were raised with strong family bonds to the water that fostered a sense of tradition critical to their self-identities. They were not drawn to the occupation so much as born into it. Thinking about Bob in the context of the literature on meaningful work, it is not hard to see how and why his effort could be so deeply purposeful for him. He was an independent-minded entrepreneur who enjoyed the outdoors and the flexibility of working for himself. Most importantly, this meant that the meaningless drag of poor management and organizational practices did not apply to his work, with the notable exception of the increasingly stringent government environmental regulations placed on his industry. His job tasks were variable, challenging, and methodical, requiring skill and precision. Operating alone on his vessel, none of his tasks could be considered pointless, as all the details are necessary to achieve his end goal of hauling lobster traps from the ocean floor. His work was significant. In Bob's case, he lacked vessel mates, so interpersonal relationships neither challenged nor accentuated his sense of meaning in work. Despite the economic challenges faced by breaking even as a small operation fisher, the work itself had many of the hallmarks of a meaningful work experience. It is no wonder that Bob and others ignored the fishing risk with such a strong sense of meaning and purpose driving their daily work efforts.

Darlene the supervisor had a completely different work environment than Bob. She was not the captain of her own ship, and her low-wage job required no formal education or skills training. Darlene's family pedigree did not direct her toward a career in convenience store management; it was a job that paid the bills. The store she managed was part of a family-owned local chain of convenience stores with a level of familiarity between the managers, owners, and employees. As a small operation, it lacked many of the organizational no-no's that can plague meaningless work environments. Darlene's work ethic and knack for efficiency were recognized quickly under the tight-knit organizational structure. When I reflect back on my experience learning under Darlene's supervision, she was someone who valued her effort in the moment but often spoke of her aspirations of going back to school. Doing a good job had direct and important meaning to her, but what seemed to sustain Darlene was her eye on the future. Meaningful work for Darlene was a highly personal experience that was facilitated by an open and welcoming small organizational structure that valued her contribution, work ethic, and efficiency.

One thing is clear from the literature on meaningful work and the countless examples of its expression in individual workers. Meaningful work is not a one-size-fits-all experience. It is highly personal, and each worker will experience the same combination of factors that impede or promote meaningful work in different ways. For Bob, it was defined by a sense of independence, tradition, and being the master of his own destiny. For Darlene, doing a job well gave meaning in the moment, while her aspirational goals and a friendly work environment helped her derive meaning from an otherwise undesirable job.

MEANINGFUL WORK IN THE AGE OF COVID

According to the BLS, workers are quitting their jobs in numbers not seen since data collection began in 2000.[38] Nearly 3 percent (over four million) of US workers voluntarily quit their jobs in August 2021, doubling the quit rate over just a year and a half. Unlike previous spikes in the quit rate, the Great Resignation has been experienced as an economy-wide phenomenon with broad-reaching effects across business sectors, geographic regions, and firm sizes.[39] Typically, during periods of economic uncertainty like recessions, fewer Americans will voluntarily leave their job, not more. The historically low quit rates observed during the Great Recession of 2008–2009 reflect this standard trend. Although the present economy does not meet the definition of a recession at the time of this writing, there are many worry signs and uncertainties related to inflation, supply shortages, the pandemic, and global conflict that would typically give pause to workers considering shifting jobs. Not so in the current labor market, where 71 percent of US and Canadian workers surveyed in a recent Gallup Poll reported that it was actually a good time to find a job.[40] The Great Resignation is indicative of a paradigm shift in the labor market, a fundamental change in the expectations for how work will contribute to a more integrated experience of well-being.

Using the terminology outlined in this book, workers may be seeking employment that will contribute holistically to their affective, evaluative, and eudaemonic well-being. They want to be satisfied with their day-to-day interactions with work, have it contribute to their overall satisfaction in life, and have it help derive meaning and purpose from their existence. A soul-searching of sorts is underway, with workers striving to identify and secure meaningful work experiences that will complement their lives. Similar to the example of nurses opting out of direct patient care, meaningful work expressions and sentiments weigh heavily on these quit decisions. Workers who identify their jobs with meaning and purpose are more rooted and satisfied in their work than those who assign higher values to attributes such as workload and pay. High rates of quitting are indicative of a shift in priorities for the modern-day worker, including a desire for meaningful work.

Workers are changing jobs in search of better opportunities that are more connected with their priorities and life goals; meanwhile, the ground is shifting under them in ways that will significantly alter how they construct meaning and purpose for themselves in the workplace. The Great Resignation is destined to be a short-term phenomenon as the labor market eventually settles out toward a new and steadier equilibrium state. But the drastic changes in the physical dimensions of work brought about by the pandemic point to an altogether new horizon for the nature of work. According to a recent labor report, 20–25 percent of workers in advanced economies could work remotely three-plus days a week on a long-term basis without any loss in productivity.[41] Growth in e-commerce has surged to record levels, with a steep rise in the reliance on digital platforms; automation, artificial intelligence, and robotic processes have accelerated in work areas that previously required a high degree of physical proximity. No doubt, the pandemic has brought elevated attention to the physical dimension of work. In fact, work with the highest physical proximity and level of human interaction before the pandemic have experienced the most change from it.

The new normal presents some workers the opportunity to balance their personal and work lives by avoiding stressful commutes, allowing more flexible work schedules, and providing a home life that is otherwise untethered to the physical location of work. The proliferation of e-commerce saves workers time by replacing time-intensive efforts to shop with the ease of home delivery. Automation and artificial intelligence technologies can serve a similar purpose to make tasks quicker and easier, freeing workers up for leisure activities that may enhance their quality of life.

However, all of these new conveniences are not without a cost. The reduced physicality of work drives a wedge between those interpersonal relationships that can be so critical to the experience of meaningful work. Supportive coworkers, service to others, and those chance encounters that break the work monotony are harder to simulate in a remote setting. Automation of job tasks with the intent to save time might leave workers saddled with boring and pointless tasks that can so often lead to worker apathy and turnover. The push toward virtual work may ultimately lead to the normalization of an existential labor market whereby the true meaningful work experience is left to the history books.

Although this sort of dystopian labor market that cuts all but essential workers off from the physicality of work may never fully materialize, it is important to recognize the potential drawbacks of the time-saving flexibility of that new normal. And undoubtedly, the reduced physicality of labor is likely to impact different segments of workers differently. A recent report predicts that nearly 30 percent of US workers in low-wage direct service industries will need retraining and new occupations if the pandemic era shifts to remote work, e-commerce, and automation continue as the new normal.[42] Like most labor market shocks, the job losses from the reduced physicality of labor will not be felt uniformly across the population but will disproportionately impact low-wage, young, uneducated, female, and minority workers who are overrepresented in the affected service industries.

SUMMARY

This chapter investigates the concept of meaningful work as a key ingredient to worker health and well-being. A general sense of meaning and purpose in life, also known as eudaemonic well-being, has been linked with positive health benefits, longevity, and enhanced quality of life. Meaningful work narrows the concept of eudaemonic well-being to describe jobs that enhance physical, cognitive, and emotional energy in return for work deemed valuable and worthwhile. The story of twentieth-century nuns in the United States provides an excellent example of the benefits of meaningful work in action. Nuns were afforded access to meaningful work experiences long before women were accepted into the labor force. It is no small coincidence that they lived significantly longer and healthier lives than non-nun women of their generations.

The study of meaningful work crosses many disciplinary boundaries, and there is no one definitive factor or antecedent that predicts meaningful work. It is very much an individual experience felt differently by each worker, varying even within individuals over space and time. Workers are more likely to experience meaningful work when they connect to multiple diverse sources of meaning as opposed to a single or narrow concept of meaningful work. Job tasks that are challenging, creative, and variable; supportive workplace relationships across the range of peer and power dynamics; organizational structures that are community oriented and encourage teamwork; management styles that are supportive and foster open communication; and a work environment that prioritizes work-life balance are some of the many important features of jobs where a sense of meaning and purpose can thrive. Importantly, research suggests that meaningful work cannot be manufactured by an organization, but its foundations can be degraded by poor management practices that reduce the opportunities for individual employees to connect in meaningful ways with their work lives. Put a bit differently, organizations cannot make your work meaningful, but they can make it meaningless.

The pandemic presents some unique challenges to the traditional ways in which meaningful work has been experienced and accessed by workers in the past. The reduced physicality of work and move toward virtual and remote work settings may have important downstream consequences for how workers connect with and experience meaning from their work. Although the drive toward remote work may align initially with work-life balance goals and interests in new opportunities and challenges, it may ultimately drive a wedge between the worker and the supportive relationships, institutions, and spaces that are so critical to fostering meaningful work.

JOB STRESS AND BURNOUT

The man whose whole life is spent in performing a few simple operations, of which the effects are perhaps always the same, or very nearly the same, has no occasion to exert his understanding or to exercise his invention in finding out expedients for removing difficulties which never occur. He naturally loses, therefore the habit of such exertion, and generally becomes as stupid and ignorant as it is possible for a human creature to become.
—Adam Smith

A CAUTIONARY TALE

When Cheryl's company switched to a permanent work-from-home policy after more than a year of temporary remote work during the initial stages of the pandemic, she was quick to embrace the change. After more than twenty years working as an insurance claims specialist for the same company, she was confident that she could be just as productive at managing cases from home as she was in the office. Although she missed socializing with friends and colleagues after the switch to fully remote, the new flexibility outweighed the lost in-person connection with her peers. She happily shed her work attire in favor of comfy clothes and sweatpants, created a home work space out of her spare bedroom, and replaced her commute with morning walks. The welcome change initially had a positive impact overall on work-life balance for Cheryl as well as on two of her work colleagues who I also interviewed while writing this book.

By all accounts, Cheryl is a model employee. Her peers describe her as friendly and eager to please, as someone who does not like to make waves and avoids the spotlight. Her job is not particularly challenging but does require a significant amount of training along with a confident grasp of company policy and relevant insurance regulations. Although she is not irreplaceable, it would require years of training for a replacement to gain the institutional and professional knowledge that Cheryl regularly provides to her employer, especially given her long tenure at the company.

But her remote work honeymoon was short lived. Within about four to six months after the switch to remote work, Cheryl's employer began chipping away at the flexibility and autonomy employees had previously enjoyed during the early days of the pandemic as well as during the in-office days. The once collaborative approach where efficiency targets were based on direct productivity measures, such as the number of claims processed, was replaced by surveillance software that tracked and reprimanded employees for excessive "idle time." While in the office, workers could make independent decisions about taking a break to use the restroom, get a cup of coffee, talk to a peer, and so forth. But in the new remote work environment, these independent decisions were upended by tracking apps that notified employers when the computer mouse and keyboard were not sufficiently engaged during the workday.

These comparatively rigid metrics based on continual effort instead of actual output began to take a toll on employees, especially people pleasers like Cheryl. Employees were regularly scolded for not moving their mouses or clicking their keyboards enough, two measures monitored by the company systems and used to judge what they considered to be indicators of excessive idle time. This was particularly hard on Cheryl. She was sensitive to negative attention and critique from managers and preferred to avoid conflict at all costs.

Many of Cheryl's peers devised ways to beat the medieval idle time rules by installing workarounds that would periodically move the mouse or rhythmically press a single key on the keyboard. A quick search of the internet will net many results for these so-called mouse movers or jigglers as well as automatic keyboard "clickers." But Cheryl opted to do things the old-fashioned way and responded to calls by her manager to reduce idle time by manually moving the mouse and clicking the keyboard as needed to reduce her recorded idle time. Cheryl is a rule follower, not a rule breaker. So she did as she was told.

After about one year of remote work under the idle time policy, Cheryl started her Wednesday workday like any other. She got up, donned her work-from-home uniform of t-shirt and shorts, and got to the business of claims management, clicking, and jiggling. But she was not feeling well that morning. She had been experiencing chest pain for a few days that she attributed to heartburn and had treated accordingly. But the sharp pain in her chest just did not want to go away. At sixty-one years old, Cheryl was in excellent health and always had been. She worked through milder pain on Monday and Tuesday, but by the Wednesday workday, it was all she could do to periodically jiggle the mouse and click a key so as not to draw the ire of her boss. She accomplished no claims management that day, just a whole lot of clicking and jiggling to avoid being flagged for idle time. Three weeks prior, Cheryl's manager had scolded her over her idle time numbers and warned that an employee had just been fired for the same offense. So, she clicked and jiggled through increasingly intense chest pain.

Like all employees at the company, Cheryl had access to paid time off (PTO), and those requests had to be approved by management. But managers were often critical of employee requests for PTO and would frequently override ones they determined to be nonessential. Cheryl had been recently warned by her direct supervisor that excessive use of PTO, even PTO that she was entitled to by employment contract, could be grounds for dismissal. And according to her colleagues, the use of sick time is even more taboo than PTO at this company. In the remote work environment, employees were just not supposed to get sick.

So even though the pain was certainly bad enough that Wednesday for Cheryl to go to the doctor, she settled on calling her doctor instead, which she could do without leaving her primary task that day to click and jiggle. Not surprisingly, based on her persistent symptoms, the doctor immediately recommended she go to an emergency room. But Cheryl was in a bind. She could not ask for her earned PTO without fear of retaliation, sick time was out of the question, and she could not risk the idle time. After more than two decades working for the same company, she felt that her job was in jeopardy. So, she ignored the doctor's advice and kept clicking and jiggling through the pain. She somehow managed to click and jiggle her way to 4:30 p.m., the end of her workday, despite intense pain. She remained perfectly still at her desk throughout the day except for small movements of her hands, because even a minor shift in her position or larger body movement was accompanied by intense pain.

Cheryl's colleague Sandy recounts a day filled with worry and fear for her friend. Sensing there was something wrong, she tried unsuccessfully to get her to go to the doctor. But Sandy, like Cheryl, was all too familiar with the anxiety and fear of retaliation associated with asking for PTO or unscheduled time off as a sick day. She herself had been recently admonished for requesting PTO to celebrate her own birthday. And on another recent occasion, she was required to document a widespread internet outage near her home to justify a brief increase in idle time. So Sandy was no stranger to the company policy of micromanagement and distrust. Ultimately, all she could do was stay in constant contact with Cheryl by phone and text and make sure that she got medical attention when the end of that long workday finally came.

By the time Cheryl got to the hospital that evening, the doctors told her that she had had a heart attack. In fact, she likely had that heart attack during that very workday while she was clicking and jiggling away to avoid punishment by her managers. Cheryl ultimately received triple bypass surgery and spent three months recovering from the episode before being able to return to work. When Sandy tried to raise awareness with company management about Cheryl's near-death experience with idle time, the manager told Sandy that it was Cheryl's family history of heart disease that was to blame and not company policy. How the company was aware of Cheryl's family medical history, Sandy did not know. But management was clearly unaware that Cheryl had in fact been part of a closed adoption at birth, and so her known family history was irrelevant to this heart attack in an otherwise healthy woman in her sixties. Although still wary about making sure to click and jiggle so as not to draw the ire of her managers, Cheryl is more cautious now about balancing her job stress and health. When I interviewed Cheryl months after the episode, I could still hear the fear of retaliation in her voice.

According to a 2022 survey by the American Psychological Association, slightly more than half of US workers report being electronically monitored or tracked by their employers while they work. In tracked versus nontracked employees, 60 versus 35 percent feel tense or stressed during the workday, 45 versus 22 percent believe their work negatively impacts their mental health, and 23 versus 13 percent consider their workplaces somewhat or very toxic, respectively.[1]

Cheryl and Sandy both value their ability to work from home. They consider it a key benefit to the job along with the competitive wages and bonuses offered by this company. So, in many ways the post-COVID work adjustments have proved beneficial to Cheryl and her colleagues by providing work location flexibility. But the proliferation of policies on worker surveillance and monitoring, as well as micromanagement of work time, is contributing to an increase in work-related stress and negative well-being for susceptible employees like Cheryl. It also contributes to a culture of distrust between employees and managers. According to Sandy, "we're treated like the enemy now and it wears you down."

Cheryl's case also points out the perils of presenteeism, otherwise known as working while you are sick. In the work-from-home setting, she and her colleagues were strongly discouraged from taking sick days. In fact, Cheryl had received a clear message from her manager the week prior that regular use of sick time, regardless of whether it was technically allowed under her employment contract, could be grounds for dismissal. As a result, Cheryl chose to continue working through a heart attack for fear of reprisal from her bosses. But she was not at all productive that day. It was truly a day of lost work for her employer as she focused all her efforts on jiggling and clicking her way through the pain.

Cheryl's case is not unique. Presenteeism contributes to both ill-health of workers and lost productivity for employers across the globe. Workers who feel presenteeism is their only option experience greater levels of job insecurity and higher levels of stress and job strain compared to those with more supportive absence and leave policies.[2] Research suggests that presenteeism is responsible for more productivity loss than actually being absent from work.[3] Although not the entire picture, presenteeism and its antecedents are among the many factors driving the extraordinarily high economic cost of work-related stress across the globe.[4] The vast majority of productivity lost to pain-related conditions in the US workforce has been traced to presenteeism, not absenteeism.[5]

Another important management concept at play in Cheryl's work environment is the idea of psychological safety. Management scientist Amy Edmondson describes psychological safety in the workplace as a space where employees can freely express their concerns, ask questions, share ideas, and make mistakes without fear of retaliation or humiliation.[6] A psychologically safe environment is one that fosters interpersonal risk taking, trust, and candor. In a 2023 meta-analysis of the psychological safety literature, Edmondson links years of research on the topic to a wide range of positive management outcomes, including work performance, creativity, and error reporting.[7] Cheryl's workplace represents a worst-case scenario that combines low psychological safety with high performance standards, which, according to Edmondson, fosters an environment of heightened anxiety, stress, and mental health strain on workers.

PHYSIOLOGY OF STRESS

In more ways than one, our bodies are a byproduct of our early ancestors' encounters with work. Over tens of thousands of years, natural selection favored humans who were adept at staying alive, and work was a matter of confronting daily threats. We adapted in physical size and strength to hunt or flee, developed fine motor skills and dexterity to fashion tools and engage in agriculture, and expanded higher brain functions to make choices that informed our survival at a time when it was our main job.

Over the span of human history, our bodies developed a sophisticated and intricate system of dealing with life-threatening stressors, also known as the fight-or-flight response. Our nervous systems developed to react swiftly to dangers, to give us a jolt of energy and instinct at just the right moment. Humans who were the best at engaging the fight-or-flight response were more likely to survive and pass on their genes to the next generation. This evolution of the human stress reaction occurred over tens of thousands of years during a time when there was little distinction between survival and work. You worked to survive, and you survived to work. Fast forward to the modern-day work environment where those ancient confrontations with life or death are relatively rare, replaced instead by a work environment over which many workers have little control. Leading job scientist Robert Karasek and his colleague Töres Theorell put it this way: "We still have roughly the same physiological response mechanisms as our hunter-gatherer ancestors, and therefore the ungraspable aspects of modern work create a biologically very abnormal situation."[8]

A very abnormal situation indeed. It is interesting to dig a little deeper into the science and biology of our stress response to understand how the modern-day work environment triggers us. The autonomic nervous system (ANS) is the involuntary and largely unconscious network of nerves connecting the various systems and organs in our body back to the anchors of our brain and spinal cord. This system keeps our heart beating and our breathing steady, moves food through our intestines, and, yes, tightly controls our reactions to stress. Early stress research by Hans Selye identified a three-patterned biological response to stress, which he coined the general adaptation syndrome.[9] In response to a stressor, the ANS activates the release of chemicals that jump-start the body's physiological reaction, increasing both the heart rate and blood pressure. At this stage, vital functions like circulation and breathing are prioritized over less immediate concerns such as metabolism, digestion, and waste removal. In this state of short-term-heighted awareness, the body is self-protective but out of balance. To restore balance once the threat has subsided (or the body is adapting to sustained stress), the ANS activates the release of counter chemicals that draw down the initial response. In the end, the body systems either recover and restore themselves or become depleted and overwhelmed, resulting in death. Fatal heart attacks, strokes, or shock-related deaths brought on by the body's reaction to stress or trauma are examples of the latter.

The activation and deactivation of the body in response to stress is also known as allostasis. Too much exposure to allostasis over time can change the body's internal rhythms and hormonal and metabolic processes, ultimately leading to disease. The most significant stress-related health effect in the US population is the dysregulation of internal body systems known as metabolic syndrome. Metabolic syndrome includes a cluster of conditions (high blood pressure, high cholesterol, hyperglycemia, and obesity) that are leading risk factors for the number one cause of death in the United States—heart disease—and contributes to type 2 diabetes and stroke. Research suggests that long-term exposure to stress, and most significantly work-related stress, contributes to metabolic syndrome at a level on par with physical inactivity.[10] For example, in a prospective study of British workers, employees subjected to chronic work stress experienced double the odds of developing metabolic syndrome compared to those without work stress.[11] Metabolic syndrome is a critical disease pathway leading to chronic heart disease, and job stress represents both a direct and indirect risk by increasing negative behaviors that contribute to heart disease like poor diet, nicotine and alcohol abuse, and lack of exercise.[12]

This complicated reactive system of interconnected nerves and organs appropriately prioritized survival in our ancestors when the odds were against us. But the odds are no longer against us. A baby girl born in the United States today is expected to live into her early eighties and die from cancer or heart disease, not from a brush with a saber tooth tiger. Deaths from accidents and injuries that might necessitate a primordial fight-or-flight response are now thankfully rare. Deaths on the job have also dropped precipitously, even in high-risk occupations like commercial fishing.

STRESS IN THE WORKPLACE

So, in this twist of Darwinian fate, our bodies are biologically primed to overrespond to stress and engage the fight-or-flight response when neither of those actions are truly necessary. We also know that jobs play an outsized role in triggering the body's stress cycle and increase our risk of disease over time, particularly metabolic syndrome and chronic heart disease.[13] In short, stress at work can exhaust our natural ability to maintain physiological balance of our internal systems.

The early work by Robert Karasek discussed in chapter 1 on the job strain model emphasized mental strain at work as a balance between the demands of the job and a worker's control to decide how to meet those demands.[14] More specifically, job-related mental strain occurs most often when the demand is high but the control is low. Karasek's work was groundbreaking at the time because previous job stress models focused either on job demand or job control, ignoring the interplay between the two factors. Karasek aptly noted that some very high-demand jobs do not result in undue mental strain, while some very low-demand, simple jobs cause significant strain. He recognized a category of "active" jobs where inordinately high job demands are balanced by a level of autonomy to make decisions about how to manage those demands at the worker level.

Karasek was a proponent of redesigning jobs, particularly high-demand jobs, to provide more decision latitude to workers as a way to reduce job strain and the negative health and well-being outcomes associated with it. He suggested that redesigning jobs to emphasize control would improve worker health while not negatively impacting output levels, which may be the case if the solution focused simply on reducing job demands. Karasek's early model eventually became known as the job-demand-control model and was later adapted to include social support in the workplace (job-demand-control-support model). The expanded model recognized the important role of social supports as a modifying factor in job strain; that is, for any given job-demand-control balance, those working in low-support settings experienced higher rates of disease and poorer health than workers in high-support settings.[15]

Subsequent research on the job strain model has put more emphasis on support and resources over autonomy or decision latitude in balancing out stressful job demands leading to mental strain and ultimately burnout.[16] Another derivative of the job strain model focused on the imbalance between work effort and reward, pointing to high job strain in cases with high effort yet low perceived reward.[17] Ultimately, the extent to which job demands versus control versus supports factor into the outcome of job strain will vary by occupation, worker, and situation.

HISTORICAL PERSPECTIVES ON THE EROSION OF WORKER CONTROL
We can trace the de-evolution of worker control and resulting uptick in job strain back a century to an influential book that laid the foundation for the field of industrial engineering and efficiency management. In his 1911 publication, *The Principles of Scientific Management*, Frederick Taylor touted a solution to respond to the challenges of his day by solving what he termed the "national efficiency" crisis.[18] According to Taylor, inefficiencies perpetuated by society and industry were creating an alarming scarcity of resources that he considered to be unsustainable. Taylor argued that businesses relied too heavily on the intellect and skill of the individual worker, who he considered to be inefficient.

Taylor proposed a systems- as opposed to human-centric approach to production, one that was designed with a single goal in mind—efficiency. His systems-based approach, known as scientific management or Taylorism, used engineering calculations to break down job tasks into their simplest and most repetitive forms, with an end goal to increase worker efficiency and reduce idle time. Extraneous movements were eliminated as inefficient to the process, speeding the pace of work. Downtime was engineered out of the workday, reducing worker idle time to a bare minimum. The work became less physical since unnecessary body mechanics and movements were eliminated from the process. Taylorized workplaces shunned social connections among workers and, when possible, physically isolated them from each other. Managers represented the top of the decision food chain and designed the workflow pattern. Skilled workers were replaced by a secondary class of low-skilled laborers who were trained to execute their small contribution to the production process.

Scientific management revolutionized the production process and succeeded in achieving Taylor's desired productivity gains. But it also perpetuated an unnatural shift in job stress and increased psychological demands on workers who now lacked decision latitude and social supports. Formerly active jobs were replaced with passive and psychologically demanding work. Based on these side effects of Taylorism, Karasek surmised that the shift in the balance of decision-making power from workers to managers was ultimately a net financial drain on the economy.[19] In other words, increased efficiency was offset by negative health and well-being outcomes from increased mental strain on workers. These management practices have been framed by some advocates as "social pollution," with poor health externalized to workers while the productivity gains accrued only to employers. Likened to the environmental movement, some have called for reprioritizing the work environment for health as a matter of human sustainability.[20]

So, long before Cheryl's bosses put in place their idle time strategy, Taylor focused on designing the manufacturing production process to increase the pace of work and, yes, to reduce pesky idle time! Although initially designed with manufacturing in mind, modern surveillance technologies have made it possible to track and eliminate idle time for remote service industry workers like Cheryl. The gig economy represents another technology-based derivative of modern-day scientific management, characterized by low-skilled, low-paid work with compensation tied to the number of completed jobs. Gig work incentivizes speed at the expense of employee breaks and downtime, and provides minimal to no worker control over the pace of work or choice of gigs.

PSYCHOSOCIAL WORKPLACE HAZARDS

When we think of risky jobs, we often consider those with tangible risks of accident, injury, or death, the kind that could (theoretically) be promptly reported to authorities. The most visible of these are the outdoor and physically strenuous occupations, such as commercial fishing, farming, construction, and logging. In fact, US job protection laws are designed to shield workers from unnecessary exposure to just these types of well-characterized physical risks. The Occupational Safe and Health Act of 1970, which institutionalized worker protection in this country, has succeeded in lowering the countable numbers of accidents and injuries in these active professions over the last fifty years. In tandem, the outsourcing of more dangerous factory work to the developing world has further served to reduce physical hazards to US workers.

Let us consider again for a moment Bob the lobster fisher's long list of known physical hazards that make his job particularly risky. Topping the list are vessel disasters and falls overboard.[21] Vessel disasters are those that rise to the level of making Bob abandon ship, for example, with a fire, sinking, or capsized boat. And like his grandfather before him, Bob could fall overboard for any number of reasons. One wrong move or rogue wave could land even the most skilled lobster fisher in the cold water. The heavy and mobile equipment also present a risk to Bob, especially if he gets entangled in the ropes or struck by a lobster trap as it propels off the deck. No doubt, the risks all lead to one dangerous result—with Bob in the water. For that reason, he can reduce his risks tremendously by wearing a personal flotation device. It also helps if he keeps his vessel and safety equipment properly maintained, including a survival suit that would protect him from frigid waters. The laws mandate various levels of precautions depending on the vessel's size and how far from shore a fisher operates, but following the precautions is largely at the discretion of Bob and his peers. When I met Bob, he was operating the vessel alone, was not wearing a personal flotation device, and his vessel and equipment were out of compliance with US Coast Guard safety standards.

So this begs the original question presented in the introduction: why would Bob ignore these risks and continue lobster fishing when there are clearly other less risky professions available to him on the mainland? It is not a particularly lucrative occupation for small operators like Bob, who often struggle to stay afloat year after year with market fluctuations in the price of lobster balanced against increasing regulatory pressures and the cost of bait, fuel, and vessel maintenance. The fact that Bob was fishing alone suggests that his bottom line could not support the added cost of cutting a crew member into a share of his catch. The tasks are physical and require strength, precision and repetition, especially for those fishers like Bob who are alone on their vessels. Fishers must also be expert navigators and mechanics to do their jobs well and avoid accidents. Not surprisingly, Maine requires all new lobster fishers to go through a two-year-long formal apprenticeship program before they can start out on their own. But despite all this, Bob was satisfied with his job. In fact, he could not imagine himself doing anything else.

And then there's Cheryl. Working for the same insurance company for nearly twenty-five years, there is little physical risk to being an insurance agent beyond the less acute ergonomic hazards related to poor posture,

inactivity, and too much sitting. Yet the heavy-handed management policies have placed significant demands on employees, especially people pleasers like Cheryl, who now face minute-by-minute micromanagement that
has eliminated a sense of personal control over the pace and pattern of
work effort.

We can look to the job strain model to understand Bob and Cheryl's
overall job risks. According to Karasek, Bob's job is "active" as opposed
to "passive," one that is challenging and demanding yet balanced with a
high degree of autonomy to make decisions and use his professional judgment as an expert fisher.[22] Karasek argued that these sorts of active jobs, and
particularly those that require physical exertion like fishing, are actually
protective of the psychological strain that results from more passive jobs.
In contrast, Cheryl's job is very passive, requiring her to spend hours on
end at a desk working on insurance claims. According to Karasek, these
types of passive jobs where employees perceive the stress and stakes to be
high but exert little to no control over their pattern of work can exacerbate
strain on workers. If we view the totality of Bob's occupational risks, we
must balance the tangible risk of accident or injury against the health protective features that his active job provides in terms of reducing his risk of
psychological strain. Bob's stated ignorance of his personal risk of accident
or injury on the job seems less irrational when weighed against the lower
risk of psychological strain the characteristics of his occupation provide
him, especially compared to Cheryl. The fact that Bob runs his own show
as self-employed compared to company workers like Cheryl may also tip
the balance in his favor. Research predicts lower levels of job stress, illness, and sick days in the self-employed as a result of higher job autonomy
and control.[23]

Despite significant progress over the last fifty years to reduce unnecessary exposure to physical workplace hazards like Bob's, Cheryl's case highlights the many silent risks to workers that are more difficult to count and
characterize; not surprisingly, government regulations that protect workers are behind the curve in addressing the psychosocial hazards of the modern workplace. Yet this less visible, prolonged exposure to chronic stress
represents a major pathway toward disease and injury at work. Just as the
cutting table in the sweatshop represents an imminent danger of losing a
hand to the blade, we can think of chronic exposure to job stress as a similar
health loss by a thousand tiny cuts. But what creates an imbalance of job

strain for one worker may be less so for another, depending on the underlying skill set, temperament, and physical and mental health baseline. At Cheryl's company, not all workers handled the new job stress as hard as she did. Many developed workarounds to reexert control over their daily work routines. As silly as it sounds, those automatic keyboard clickers and mouse jigglers were health promoting for Cheryl's peers.

HEALTH EFFECTS FROM CHRONIC JOB STRAIN

Research on various aspects of the work environment that ultimately lead to chronic disease have identified many linkages worth considering "risky" on par with the more visible physical hazards. The strongest and most long-standing evidence pointing to negative health effects of job stress are an increased risk of heart disease, likely through the pathway of higher incidence of metabolic syndrome as noted previously.[24] In a recent meta-review of the existing science, high job demand was also associated with increased risk of stroke, diabetes, and depression. An effort-reward imbalance was associated with heart disease, while job insecurity was associated with depression, anxiety, psychotropic medication use, and diabetes. Long working hours were associated with heart disease, stroke, obesity, and depression.[25]

Another meta-analyses of the role of job stressors on worker health explored thirty-two studies, linking low job control with a 21 percent higher all-cause mortality and a 50 percent higher heart disease mortality compared to workers with high job control.[26] Job stress can also play an important role in chronic low back pain, which impacts more than one in five worldwide and represents the leading cause of early retirement.[27] The imbalance of high job demand and low job control work settings has been linked to an increased usage of sick days in a number of studies.[28] Workers with preexisting mental health disorders are particularly vulnerable to job strain and as such use even higher rates of sick time in high-stress work environments relative to their peers.[29] The combination of high job demands and personal life stressors can be particularly detrimental to a worker's mental health and has been associated with increased future use of psychiatric mediations.[30]

A recent pair of studies by Joel Goh and colleagues examined the role of ten major workplace stressors on mortality and health-care costs in the United States, benchmarking them against the baseline risks from exposure

to secondhand smoke.[31] They found that low job control had the most significant impact on mortality of all the examined risk factors (including secondhand smoke), while high job demands had a similarly outsized impact
on mental health and morbidity compared to the other known risk factors.
In total, they linked more than 120,000 excess deaths per year in the United
States to these workplace risk factors, amounting to a total cost of 5–8
percent of annual health-care expenditures. Although it is challenging to
disentangle the myriad of health effects related to poorly constructed and
stressful work environments from other contributing factors, evidence suggests it ranks high among the leading causes of death in the United States.[32]
Of particular harm are low-control workplaces like Cheryl faced at her
insurance company.

Job stress related to gig work has also been defined in terms of the job-
demand-control model, with mixed reviews depending on the category of
worker. On the one hand, platform-dependent workers who rely on gig
work as their primary source of income will experience the demands of
the job differently and are particularly vulnerable to the precarious aspects
of the job including unpredictable work schedules, job insecurity, and low
wages. In a study of Canadian workers, platform-dependent gig workers
were at greater risk of psychological distress when compared to nondepen-
dent workers as well as wage workers and the self-employed. The primary
source of elevated stress was attributed to income precarity. The limited
gig evidence suggests that even within a given occupation where some
workers enjoy a high degree of autonomy, flexibility, and control, individual worker vulnerabilities can tip the balance of the job control scale
toward higher levels of job strain and elicit negative health and well-being
outcomes.[33]

BURNOUT

When I reflect back on my time in law enforcement, one thing that stands
out more than anything for me is how quickly I became disillusioned and
dissatisfied with the work. First and foremost, the job was exhausting.
Long hours on my feet, forced overtime, and the intermittent fear of danger punctuated by long periods of boredom took a toll on my mind and
body. The job was emotionally draining and required constant contact with
an oftentimes agitated public. While I had the discretion to stop, search,

and detain anyone crossing the border, I still felt powerless. The disproportionate focus on searching women of color encouraged by supervisors at the time put me in direct conflict with my value system. Although I started the job with a sense of adventure and eye toward the greater good, those feelings quickly faded as the reality of the job I was actually tasked with set in. Many officers were able to keep up the grueling pace and derive job satisfaction from their frontline roles in the War on Drugs, but I could not see that bigger picture. In my very first real job out of undergraduate school, I crashed and burned. Fortunately, for me that initial experience was not indicative of a larger trend of dissatisfaction with the working world. But it was in fact my first and hopefully last experience with burnout.

The World Health Organization recognizes burnout as an "occupational phenomenon," differentiating it from a medical condition.[34] It describes the work-related syndrome as the result of overwhelming, unmanaged, and chronic job stress. Not surprisingly, the science around burnout shares many key features of the models of job strain (job-demand-control-support) described previously. But a worker can theoretically experience job strain without it ultimately leading to burnout and vice versa. For many workers, unmanageable job strain can eventually lead to burnout, especially in certain people-facing industries.

Research by Christina Maslach and colleagues identified the three primary dimensions of burnout as emotional exhaustion, detachment and depersonalization, and a sense of ineffectiveness or lack of accomplishment.[35] Maslach described burnout in her seminal 1982 book as a syndrome defined by the chronic emotional stress of "people work."[36] The subsequent Maslach Burnout Inventory is the standard tool for measuring the risk and presence of burnout across these three dimensions of exhaustion, detachment, and ineffectiveness and has been the subject of thorough psychometric validation over the last forty years.[37] Questions about how often workers feel emotionally drained by work, whether they feel callous toward people, or have difficulty handling problems calmly, among a laundry list of others questions, help identify low to severe cases of burnout and have been used in the United States and across the globe to identify trends across workers and industries. My own burnout experience spans all three dimensions. I was certainly exhausted, physically and mentally. I had to detach from my natural source of empathy to stay alert and safe and ultimately perform the job tasks dictated by my supervisors. Even when

I would make an arrest or stop drugs from crossing the border, I lacked a sense that I was contributing to the greater good.

But where exactly do these feelings leading to burnout come from? Not surprisingly, research over the years have identified work overload (high job demands) as well as low job control as primary contributors to burnout. Other important factors leading to burnout include role conflict, role ambiguity, effort-reward imbalance, lack of feedback, misaligned values, and lack of support. In terms of support, treatment by supervisors is the most important predictor of burnout, while a supportive work community of colleagues has also been shown to be a critical factor.[38] In a pandemic-era study of frontline health-care workers, those who identified more strongly as members of a team reported significantly less stress and burnout on the job.[39] The findings suggest that feelings of inclusivity and group belonging may buffer workers against stress and burnout, especially among new, low-status, or temporary workers most likely to experience exclusion in the workplace.

Although the signs and symptoms of burnout can mirror those of other mental health conditions like anxiety and depression, burnout belongs in a class of its own. Not only is it context specific to the workplace, but it is also driven by an individual worker's relationship to a given job and work situation. In contrast, depression tends to touch all facets of a person's life, not just the work setting. For example, I experienced swift burnout in a law enforcement setting but have not had a similar experience with teaching, another high burnout profession. Not surprisingly, workers who are more prone to depression are also more likely to experience burnout.[40] Similar to depression and anxiety, burnout can result in changes in mood and concentration, fatigue, sleep, and appetite that overflow into other nonemployment aspects of a worker's life.

Early work on burnout was limited primarily to workers in the human services and health-care industries, although the scope has since grown to include many other professions. As a result of the early focus, there is a comparatively deep literature on burnout in health-care professionals such as nurses. It is difficult to overstate the role of the pandemic on the burnout status quo among these essential health-care workers. The US Surgeon General estimates that annual labor replacement costs for burnout-related turnover in the US health-care sector are more than $9 billion for nurses and $2.6–$6.3 billion for physicians.[41]

MANAGING BURNOUT

A few options exist for workers in burnout situations. They can try to change the situation if they have not fallen victim to learned helplessness, can try to alter their response to the situation, or can avoid the situation all together by quitting. Research suggests that workers who respond emotionally to problems and lack flexibility in their coping strategies are more likely to become disengaged and experience burnout.[42] Although they might try to learn strategies to reduce emotionality and inflexibility around problem solving, workers under excessive job strain are the least likely to access these sorts of health-promoting adaptive strategies. In fact, research suggests that workers under stress are more likely to experience impaired cognitive function, have a negative mood, communicate poorly, make careless mistakes, and create unnecessary interpersonal conflicts. Not surprisingly, workers tend to make bad decisions when they are stressed! They undermine themselves in ways that would make no sense to their nonstressed alter egos. Small behavioral failures in an attempt to deal with mild stressors can spiral out of control and create a negative feedback loop of poor coping that can ultimately lead to burnout.

Because of these limitations in how humans respond and make decisions under duress, many experts suggest that burnout can only be addressed with aggregate workplace strategies that do not rely on workers to adapt or change their natural inclinations. Organizational supports and strategies to improve psychosocial work conditions have been shown to be more effective and more likely to make inroads on burnout than strategies directed at individual worker behavior change.[43]

From an organizational perspective, management scientists have explored ways to redesign the work experience to reduce stress and burnout while also contributing to job satisfaction and overall well-being. Erin Kelly and colleagues identified several key management strategies aimed at improving health and well-being in the workplace,[44] a number of which focus on shifting the balance of control back to workers. This anti-Taylorist realignment of the workplace affords workers greater autonomy over the pattern and pace of their work, flexibility on when and where to do the work, increased predictability of work schedules, and the opportunity to identify and solve workplace challenges. In addition to greater job control, Kelly also suggests moderating job demands by keeping organizations adequately staffed and workloads reasonable, as well as building a sense of work community and supports that recognize the personal and work-life balance needs of workers. Notably absent from this list of managerial strategies are interventions that rely on worker behavior modifications, focusing instead on organizational-level change designed to reduce demands, increase control, and provide greater support to workers.[45]

Workplace interventions have been shown to be more effective and sustainable when they target the aggregate workplace and not the individual worker because they reach a broader population and not just individuals seeking health promotion and workplace wellness opportunities.[46] A 2019 study published in the *Journal of the American Medical Association* explored the benefits of workplace wellness programs in a randomized control trial of middle- and low-income employees in the large warehouse company BJ's.[47] Employees participating in the wellness programs self-reported a positive change in health behaviors, that is, weight management, reduced smoking, and drinking. This positive perceived health change is notable despite the fact that objective measures of health status, health-care spending, and employment outcomes such as absenteeism, tenure, and performance, did not measurably change.

Ben Laker has popularized the idea of "job crafting" as a bottom-up management approach that allows workers to redesign aspects of their own work environment to better match their interests and needs.[48] The majority of job crafting post-pandemic has focused on employee control over the amount or type of tasks performed, but Laker notes that job crafting might also include "relational crafting"—how an employee communicates and interacts with their colleagues or "cognitive crafting"—how they derive or perceive meaning in their work. In a post-COVID global survey of workers, job crafting was associated with higher levels of job and personal satisfaction. On a related theme of work environment flexibility to reduce stress, there is renewed attention post-COVID to the potential benefits of a four-day work week. Available evidence from experiments with the four-day work week across the globe suggests the potential to both enhance worker well-being and boost productivity.[49]

PANDEMIC TRENDS IN STRESS AND BURNOUT
A 2021 survey of full-time US workers showed an alarming uptick in stress and downstream mental health effects attributed to the workplace across

a two-year span covering the pandemic.[50] Over three-quarters of workers reported suffering at least one symptom of a mental health condition in the past year, up 29 percent since 2019. More than a third also noted that the condition lasted longer than usual, a 71 percent increase since 2019. The most common symptoms were burnout (56 percent), depression (46 percent), and anxiety (40 percent), all significantly higher since 2019. An overwhelming 84 percent reported at least one workplace factor had negatively affected their mental health over the past year, with the two most common being emotionally draining work (37 percent) and work-life balance (32 percent). More than three-quarters reported that their productivity was also negatively impacted by their mental health (up 61 percent since 2019). While the pandemic may have exacerbated existing mental health challenges and inequities in the workplace, according to a recent US Surgeon General's report, it also brought greater visibility and focus to issues of workplace mental health and well-being.[51]

Workers face a transformed environment of psychosocial pressures in both remote and in-person work settings as employers respond to the threat of slacking by increasing task surveillance and micromanagement of work time. Higher job demands coupled with declining control over the pace and structure of the workday undoubtedly increase worker strain, with downstream impacts to the occupational risks of metabolic syndrome and heart disease. The term quiet quitting is a trendy manifestation of burnout-related disengagement as a coping strategy to adapt to these new and extraordinary pressures. Presenteeism pressures in the remote work environment represent additional challenges to health and safety in the post-COVID workforce. While well-designed remote work has the capacity to enhance flexibility, autonomy, and a sense of control among workers, poor management practices that foster a culture of surveillance and micromanagement will likely have the opposite effect.

For many workers already experiencing job strain and burnout symptoms, the pandemic may just be the straw that broke that camel's back. In a meta-analysis of burnout studies conducted during the pandemic, burnout among health-care workers was at an all-time high of 52 percent, compared to a lower 32–34 percent in the decades leading up to the pandemic. Nurses represented the highest source of health-care workers experiencing burnout at 66 percent, scoring comparatively worse on the Maslach indices of exhaustion, depersonalization, and lack of personal accomplishment.[52] Other studies have shown that essential non-health-care workers suffered even more mental health declines during the COVID shutdown than essential health-care workers despite the latter receiving the most media attention.[53]

According to a 2021 survey, 32 percent of nurses are considering leaving direct patient care, a 10 percent increase in less than a year.[54] Ballooning job strain related to the pandemic have pushed many nurses toward retirement. The average nurse in 2020 was fifty-two years old, and bottlenecks in nursing training programs make it impossible to replace the rapidly declining numbers of nurses leaving the profession due to burnout and retirement. The growing labor supply crisis of nurses is a classic example of perils of burnout in action. Between 2019 and 2020, vacancy rates for registered nurses at hospitals in Massachusetts doubled, attributed to rapid turnover and burnout as nurses leave hospital employment for other health-care jobs or retire all together.[55] This shortage is likely to become more acute over time, especially for certain high-demand nurses such as nurse practitioners. According to the BLS, the demand for nurse practitioners is expected to grow by 40 percent over the next ten years.[56] Policies to address the nursing shortage will certainly fall short unless they tackle the work environment conditions that make these professionals especially vulnerable to burnout. Future research focused on the long-term and downstream effects of increased stress and burnout across occupations and worker demographics will be important to addressing these ongoing challenges.

Despite these alarming trends, leading management expert Lynda Gratton sees the transformed COVID workplace as a unique opportunity to renegotiate the terms of work in a way that was impossible to do before the pandemic. Gratton argues that organizations could leverage this quantum leap in work practices to produce a win-win strategy to enhance both worker well-being and business performance. In her book *Redesigning Work*, she outlines a creative management strategy to identify the underlying drivers of productivity and use them as a baseline for reimagining new patterns of work that might achieve productivity metrics in a worker-centered and balanced way.[57] Data-driven reviews of remote and hybrid work, leave policies, work-time flexibility, and many other COVID-era proliferations provide an opportunity in some cases to increase well-being without sacrificing profit margins.

SUMMARY

This chapter begins with the story of Cheryl. The heart attack at her desk could be chalked up to a random case of ill-health if not for the many contributing factors that point to her job as a major source of her cardiovascular risk. According to the job strain model, Cheryl's work would have been considered passive even before the pandemic. As an insurance agent, hers is primarily desk work that is both low in job demands but also low in decision latitude. As she and her colleagues transitioned to fully remote during the initial stages of the pandemic and then permanently a year later, what little control she had enjoyed previously to set her pace of work was eliminated by a new company culture of micromanagement and surveillance. Personal days and sick time were discouraged. Although some of her peers developed workarounds that allowed them to reexert control over their pace of effort, Cheryl's eagerness to please and anxiety over being punished left her vulnerable to job strain that ultimately overwhelmed her system. The fact that she continued to work through the heart attack is key evidence of her work as hazardous.

The original job strain model described work-related stress as a disequilibrium between the demands of a job and the control afforded to the worker to determine how to best meet those demands. Later extensions of the model incorporated various other important factors into the equation, including access to resources and a supportive work environment, a perceived imbalance between effort and reward, and work schedule predictability. High levels of job strain (high demand, low control) have been linked to a range of chronic health issues, especially cardiovascular conditions, as well as increased pain, mortality, mental health problems, time off to sick days, and presenteeism.

Burnout, characterized by emotional exhaustion, detachment, and a lack of accomplishment, is on the rise in response to the increased demands placed on many workers since the pandemic. Decades of research on burnout in certain people-facing occupations such as health care have provided a solid base of evidence for understanding the factors that have pushed a growing number of workers and occupations toward burnout over the last few years.

Research suggests that workers under stress are more likely to make bad decisions, including those impacting their health. For that reason, the epidemics of job stress and burnout are unlikely to abate if the problem is left to the individual worker to solve on their own by adapting to more stressful working conditions over time. Unprecedented levels of job switching, quitting, and retirements that have strained the labor market are evidence that workers are choosing not to adapt to burnout strain but are instead leaving those stressful work conditions for better opportunities elsewhere. For that reason, solutions to widespread stress and burnout in the post-COVID labor market will likely require active organization-level involvement and solutions to restore balance.

JOBS OF THE FUTURE

The future influences the present just as much as the past.
—Friedrich Nietzsche

Over the pages of this book, we have encountered many workers who have thrived in tough conditions. Bob the fisher's job was physically intense but ultimately satisfying, the benefits of strenuous activity, independence, and cultural supports outweighing the dangerous aspects of the job. And then there was Darlene, who was able to find meaning in dirty work with her eye on improving her lot in the future. As a group, twentieth-century nuns enjoyed access to meaningful work during a time that other women were largely cut off from it. As a consequence, they lived decades longer on average than other women of their days. Alice suffered through a transitioning economy and unemployment but came out the other side with a job better suited to her health and well-being.

We have met other workers who did not fare so well under stressful work conditions. Cheryl the insurance agent broke under the pressures of micromanagement and a culture of surveillance and clicked and jiggled her way right into a heart attack. I myself lasted less than a year as a drug cop, swiftly broken down by the physically and mentally exhausting conditions and work that oftentimes put me at odds with my moral compass. These stories have been woven into the scientific literature on work-related health and well-being to tell a broader story about jobs and the human condition. They ultimately serve to illustrate the important point that there is no one-size-fits-all approach to the science of jobs and every worker is unique in their tolerance and aptitude for difficult work.

The labor market is at a historical inflection point. New patterns of work are emerging in the post-COVID economy that have altered the landscape of physical and psychosocial occupational hazards. Workers are quitting, retiring, and changing jobs and occupations in record numbers. Job stress and burnout have skyrocketed in a few short years, leading high-skilled workers to search for jobs with better amenities like work-life balance, autonomy, and meaningful work. Meanwhile, low-skilled workers are struggling to find their place in a labor market of narrowing opportunities and new technologies that threaten to leave them behind. The pandemic has highlighted the need to understand work as a social determinant of health within the larger context of overall population health. This final chapter shifts our focus toward the future, blending the lessons learned from the science and stories in this book to describe what may lie ahead for workers.

PHYSICALITY—THE NEW OCCUPATIONAL HAZARD

An undeniable outcome of the pandemic is the heightened infection risk of being in close contact with other human beings on the job. The term "frontline worker" no longer applies just to health-care workers and emergency teams but now covers any "essential" worker who cannot work from home, including less-skilled, high-touch, and low-pay service work. Black and Brown Americans are more likely to work in these essential low-paid jobs that place them in close proximity to others. The new occupational hazard has both a short-term risk of initial COVID infection and a long-term risk associated with being among the estimated 20 percent of infected who go on to develop the long COVID symptoms of fatigue, brain fog, and shortness of breath. To further complicate matters, jobs that demand physical proximity have changed the most since the pandemic, leaving these workers to suffer both a disproportionate share of the occupational risk as well as heightened job market uncertainty. Future research to understand the interplay between the physical, emotional, and mental health risks of vulnerable essential workers is needed to promote health and well-being across the spectrum of US workers. New models of occupational risk and a shift in regulatory priorities may be needed to address the post-COVID new normal.

NOT JUST WOMEN'S WORK ANYMORE

Although women have made many strides in the labor force over the last fifty-plus years, a creeping trend is crossing the gender divide with the spread of jobs that look eerily like those done by women in the early days when their labor was devalued compared to their male peers and partners. Women's work of old was more likely to be part time, precarious, low pay, and low status. Women had less access to training and upward mobility and less power to affect change at their organizations. They also performed a disproportionate share of emotionally draining labor compared to their male counterparts. They were second-class work citizens. Fast forward to 2022, and growing segments of the labor economy are looking much like women's work of the past—precarious, part time, low pay, low status— including the gig sector and reliance on independent contractors. These new jobs share many of the hallmarks of the power imbalance that historically plagued women.

Research links many downstream consequences of productivity-linked pay for work using the gig and contract labor model to an increased risk of accident and injury, as well as a range of physical, mental, and emotional health outcomes. Other features of these jobs, like precarity, part time, and low pay, have been shown to have their own negative health and well-being effects on workers, particularly on mental health. Workers who rely on these jobs as a sole source of income, considered "platform dependent," are the most likely to suffer the ill effects and are also more likely to be young, minority, and low income. But not all workers in these sectors fall into the feminized labor force trap. Those who supplement their income with this type of work can leverage these jobs to capture the benefits of flexibility, autonomy, and work-life balance. More research is needed to understand the size and scope of the growing contract sector popularized by the gig economy to unravel these relationships, particularly as it relates to vulnerable worker populations. Current data collection efforts have been insufficient to draw causal links between this growing segment of the modern labor force and worker health and well-being.

THE DISAPPEARANCE OF LOW-SKILLED OPPORTUNITIES

More than a quarter of workers are expected to transition to totally new occupations over the next ten years on top of already historic levels of quitting, job switching, and retirements. Much of the occupational shifting is expected to occur away from low-skilled opportunities toward jobs that require a greater familiarity with technology as well as more advanced socioemotional communication skills. The transition away from low-skilled jobs places a significant retraining burden in time and expense on an otherwise low-income vulnerable segment of the US population. Over-represented in this low-skilled workforce are female, young, and minority workers as well as those without a college degree.

Declining opportunities for workers without a college degree in the pre-COVID era have been blamed for the growing health crises of "deaths of despair" or those attributed to suicide, drugs, and alcohol abuse. Ninety percent of drug overdoses in the United States occur in people without a college degree. As the labor market continues its transition toward a more technologically advanced and sophisticated service sector, those without a college degree will be left with a smaller share of an already shrinking pie. This trend has the potential to further exacerbate health inequities for this group of vulnerable workers, including in deaths of despair. Research and monitoring of the short- and long-term health and well-being of workers facing the pressures of the contraction of low-skilled work opportunities will be important to designing and implementing policy and training programs to mitigate some of the ill effects, particularly for the most vulnerable workers.

WORKERS ARE MORE THAN JUST A COG IN A MACHINE

The Great Resignation of quits, retirement, and job shifting brought on by the pandemic has revived attention on work as a source of inspiration and positive well-being. Workers who rank meaningful work as high among the preferred attributes of their job are more resilient to work-related stressors and less likely to quit. In the absence of meaning and purpose, workers face a tension to leave for opportunities that may provide a more holistic experience with work as a contributor to meaning and purpose in their broader lives. The shifting power dynamics in favor of workers in a tight labor market have provided many the opportunity to seek employment that contributes more fully to their well-being. A soul-searching of sorts is underway, with workers striving to identify and secure meaningful work experiences that will complement their lives. Looking forward, it will be important for organizations to take note of trending worker preferences around meaningful work to develop better practices and structures that provide more fertile ground for meaningful experiences. Providing workers the space to extract meaning from their work will ultimately help organizations attract and retain a productive, happy, and healthy workforce.

UNTANGLING THE ROLE OF ECONOMIC AND EMPLOYMENT TRENDS

The post-COVID economy has been a wild ride, with historic swings in unemployment, an economy teetering on the brink of a recession, and inflation at modern-day highs. Meanwhile, trends in self-employment and unionization efforts appear on the verge of reversing their long-term downward slides. This book explored the role of macroeconomic and employment conditions on worker health and well-being effects in the pre-COVID literature, and it is helpful to take a step back and look at how these relationships might predict worker outcomes in the altered economic landscape of the future.

First off, workers are typically less likely to switch jobs during periods of economic upheaval and uncertainty. Not so during the pandemic, where macroeconomic panic resulted in an uptick of quits, retirements, and job switching. The Great Resignation suggests a paradigm shift in the standard association between recessions and labor mobility, where workers take advantage of uncertainty to search for jobs that provide a more integrated experience of well-being depending on the factors most important to them. The additional safety net provided by short-term extensions and enhancements to unemployment insurance allowed many workers to ride that wave a bit longer and find a job better suited to them.

The research on recessions typically predicts a healthier population during bad economic times, although the unique circumstances of a global pandemic on health make it unlikely that a COVID-induced trough will reduce mortality. Wide swings in unemployment and uncertainty in the job market may ultimately have negative health implications for the working population, but identifying the true impact will require the perspective of time.

The health and well-being effects of the bump in retirements during the pandemic is likely to be context specific to the individual worker. Those who were forced out of meaningful and satisfying work in the downswing of the economy may be expected suffer that loss through worsening late-life health and well-being. In contrast, workers dissatisfied with their work or those in high-touch infection-risk occupations might be expected to see their health improve as a result of retirement. The literature on late-life health and well-being after retirement is ambiguous on many points and highly dependent on the underlying reasons for exiting the workforce.

As workers battle for control over their work lives, self-employment options may become more appealing to a broader base of the population. Recent upticks in the percentage of Americans who identify as self-employed seem indicative of this trend. The extent to which increasing numbers of self-employment relate to health will depend heavily on how the choice is constructed by the individual worker—to satisfy their own preferences for independent and autonomous work or out of necessity for lack of better employment options.

Although the most recent data on actual union representation continues the downward trend started many decades ago, petitions to create unions are up by 50 percent in the last year. A change of fortunes for unions may be on the horizon as workers continue to leverage their power in a tight labor market to demand better jobs. Historically, unions have not been found in the economics literature to positively impact worker health and well-being, and in fact, a large body of evidence suggests the opposite case. It is challenging to say whether more recent unionization efforts driven by a new demographic of workers in the twenty-first century may alter this relationship to demand greater and more transparent health benefits from unionization.

THE PROS AND CONS OF REMOTE WORK

Quite possibly the most striking pandemic-related change to work has been the transition from in-person to remote work for a substantial percentage of US workers. The number of US workers working from home tripled during the pandemic, with nearly one in five workers in 2021 characterized as remote by the US Census. And this is just the tip of the iceberg. Studies estimate that nearly 40 percent of US jobs could be performed entirely at home (70 percent of computer-based office work), predicting that further increases in remote work may be coming down the pike for US workers.

On the one hand, many workers are demanding remote work options from their employers, valued for its flexibility, lack of commute, reduced infection risk, and expanded choice to live outside the normal commuting distance to the office. Staying close to home and avoiding the commute has been touted by many as a boost to work-life balance, freeing up workers to engage in more leisure activities and time with family and friends. Another important perk to the worker is the fact that remote jobs tend to pay more than in-person jobs, on average. Remote work has cost advantages for many employers too, who no longer require the physical office infrastructure and related costs associated with an in-person business. Aligning the preferences of employees and employers has been made possible by advances in remote work technologies that allow the transition from in person to remote to be made without major productivity losses.

On the surface, it may appear that remote work can only be net positive for workers whose preferences align with working from home. Flexibility and the sense of control it engenders among workers is in fact one of the primary characteristics of work discussed in this book that promote health and well-being. It puts workers in the driver's seat, providing precious time and autonomy to work where (and sometimes when) they want.

But the story does not end there. Digging just a bit deeper into the structure of remote work reveals a dark underbelly that may ultimately prove health limiting. First, the reduced physicality of work drives a literal wedge of distance between workers and their colleagues, interpersonal relationships that can be so critical to the experience of meaningful work and community. Chats with supportive coworkers, opportunities to provide service to others, and chance encounters with other human beings that break the monotony of an in-person work experience are harder to simulate in the virtual work setting. The effect of cutting off workers from the socially supportive aspects of their jobs may ultimately make them more vulnerable to the effects of stress and burnout and to the wide range of health outcomes related to these conditions. Research suggests that workers are more resilient to job stressors when they derive meaning and purpose from their work, something that is harder to create in remote environments. In business terms, there is likely to be more turnover in remote versus in-person jobs.

Although the ideal scenario of remote work is one that engenders well-being through flexibility and autonomy, that has not been universally the case for many workers. First, most workers are unfamiliar with healthy workstation design and the role that ergonomic stressors play in chronic musculoskeletal conditions, particularly as they age. In addition, employers are increasingly applying the basic tenets of scientific management to their remote workforce. The origins of scientific management a century ago focused on increasing worker efficiency in manufacturing by reducing downtime and extraneous movements, cutting workers off from their peers so they can exercise direct and sustained attention to the production task. Fast forward to the remote computer-based work setup, scientific management is customized with advanced workstation surveillance technologies and micromanagement of the workday in an effort to squeeze out employee idle time and combat perceived slacking in the home work setting. These workstation surveillance technologies poke and prod a worker throughout the day to stay on task. Keystrokes and mouse movements are tracked. Breaks are regulated, lunch is regulated, and trips to the bathroom are regulated. The use of sick and personal time is discouraged, leading to presenteeism and work-life conflict. These management strategies create a job strain imbalance by increasing job demands through performance pressure while decreasing decision latitude to set the pace of the workday in what would have otherwise been a more flexible in-person work environment. According to the job-demand-control model, this will ultimately manifest in a higher risk of occupationally related chronic diseases, particularly cardiovascular conditions.

Coupled with increased virtual surveillance, many remote job tasks are engineered to be as automatic as possible to save time. Ultimately, these time-saving efficiencies may leave remote workers saddled with raw and boring tasks. It is not surprising, then, that existing evidence suggests there may be a sweet spot between remote and in-person work in the hybrid setting. Current studies indicate a U-shaped relationship between remote work and job satisfaction: satisfaction increases as more remote options are made available but then declines as a worker reaches fully remote status. Hybrid settings provide workers more flexibility in work location while also exposing them to the benefits of in-person access to colleagues and resources that help foster healthy connections and may ultimately represent the best of both worlds. More research is needed to explore the benefits of the hybrid workspace to promote health and well-being in the post-COVID economy.

REDESIGNING JOBS FOR THE FUTURE

We can think of the pandemic as a border wall of sorts between the old and new styles of work. We were all stunned when we hit that wall at full speed in the spring of 2020, woefully unprepared for the end of work as we knew it. But we have had some time to get our bearings and to find ways over and around that wall to explore a new way of working. For many workers, that means reduced physicality of the work experience and more virtual connectivity. For others, it means continued physicality but greater vulnerabilities and occupational risk. Historic levels of labor mobility show that workers are still trying to figure out what they want from jobs, testing the waters for opportunities that make their lives better, not just financially but also in terms of overall health and well-being.

Although we are facing a new normal across the spectrum of work, we can draw from the many decades of research about the characteristics of healthy and meaningful jobs to anticipate pitfalls before we stumble into them. Rethinking how we design jobs, monitor, and reward the modern-day work experience is critical to crossing that border wall to arrive in a better place than where we started, one where jobs are thoughtfully designed to enhance the human experience.

First and foremost, workers should be given more control, not less. Irregular shifts need not be so irregular. There is already a strong business case reinforcing the productivity-enhancing effect of stable scheduling. Jobs should be designed to allow for worker discretion in a way that targets productivity but does not stunt creativity and work-life balance. The principles of scientific management that proved so useful a century ago to increasing the productivity of the manufacturing workforce are not appropriate to the modern-day remote worker. This is not to say that workers should not be judged and evaluated based on their productivity. Productivity and efficiency metrics can provide transparent ways for workers to be able to benchmark their work against an expected target and self-evaluate their progress before it is flagged by a supervisor. In contrast, the spread of scientific management to the remote workplace dictates down to the keystroke how a worker should achieve that benchmark by eliminating idle time.

Better management practices that establish clear and transparent productivity benchmarks and evaluate their employees fairly and consistently based on how they meet those benchmarks will avoid unnecessary job strain and the long list of poor health and well-being outcomes that are known to accompany it. And it is a win-win. Ultimately, healthy management practices will also reduce sick days, presenteeism, worker turnover, and burnout. It is time to reverse engineer scientific management practices to reinvigorate the workforce and meet the occupational health challenges of the post-COVID economy.

There is a need to address psychosocial work hazards akin to how physical hazards have been addressed in the past. We face a much-altered landscape than we did decades ago when widescale monitoring, reporting, and regulating of workplace physical hazards became prevalent through government entities like the Occupational Safety and Health Administration and increased attention from worker unions. However, these historical efforts are behind the curve to address the diversity of psychosocial hazards workers face on the job today; the science is now sufficient to treat psychosocial conditions like the physical hazards of old. Total Worker Health initiatives that offer a holistic view of workplace hazards have moved the needle in the right direction. The explosion of remote work makes it all the more critical that we rethink the framework of physical hazards to include post-COVID psychosocial factors in a more systematic way.

The effects of turnover, burnout, presenteeism, and quiet quitting are bringing renewed attention to the important role of job stress in business profitability. Wellness programs and perks are delivered to help workers engage in health-promoting activities as a way to mitigate job stress. But this is the low-hanging fruit. Evidence shows that workers who are stressed are less likely to take advantage of wellness programs and make healthy decisions. There is no substitute for organization-level management strategies that promote healthy psychosocial working conditions as a baseline so that workers do not fall ill to job stress in the first place. For businesses that provide health insurance to their workers, poor management strategies ultimately increase company-related health-care expenses, especially when those job stressors have led to an uptick in chronic high-cost health conditions like heart disease.

A FINAL BIT OF ADVICE TO WORKERS

The tightest labor market in a generation provides a unique opportunity for workers to demand a more well-rounded existence from their workplaces and employers. This book provides a few key takeaways for workers looking to leverage their historic upper hand in today's economy.

First and foremost is the idea that more money and higher salaries are not the panacea for work struggles. That is not to say that money does not play a key role in a worker's decision to take or keep a job. Meeting basic income needs as well as relative comparisons of salary against work peers are important predictors of job satisfaction. But absolute increases in money beyond a middle-income threshold may fail to meaningfully contribute to overall happiness in the broader scheme of life. In study after study across the globe, money buys happiness up to a point, but that seemingly unquenchable thirst does more harm than good. So, if the ultimate goal is to be happy, workers have to look at the myriad of nonsalary characteristics that make a job right or wrong for them.

Depending on the individual worker, underlying personalities, skill sets, and life circumstances, these less tangible aspects of the work experience will vary in how they contribute to a sense of overall well-being. There is no single recipe to follow. Sometimes gig work can be good. Sometimes self-employment can be good, and sometimes even brief stints of unemployment can be good!

It is also important for workers to take note that job satisfaction over a work lifetime is often gained in discrete jumps from one opportunity to the next and not from staying in place. Workers as human beings are naturally risk averse to the idea of a work loss, such as unemployment. But leaning into that fear represents an important opportunity to grow and explore work that aligns with the unique characteristics both in terms of salary and nonsalary factors that will promote well-being in any individual worker.

On that chilly spring morning off the coast of Southern Maine, I thanked Bob for taking the time to talk to me about his job. I turned to make my way back to the Marine Patrol vessel, carefully straddling the gap between the two boats bobbing at opposite rhythms to the wind and ocean waves. Knowing the perils of an accidental dip in that cold water, I was mindful to hold on tight to Bob's vessel until I had a firm grip on the Marine Patrol boat alongside it. I had developed my questionnaire to be brief and streamlined in a conscious effort not to take too much of my study subjects' time. Despite the time pressure Bob faced that workday, especially with no crew to support him, he took his time with me. What should have ended after fifteen minutes went on with Bob for nearly an hour, much of it in a dialogue that stretched a simple yes or no answer into colorful stories of what made his job work for him. He shared his pride at carrying on the tradition, how it felt to be his own boss, and why he chose the work over the danger. He also shared his concerns about the increasing pressures of environmental regulations, catch limits, the price of bait, fuel, and vessel maintenance as well as the cost of purchasing and maintaining all the safety equipment that I was there to assess. Oddly, the one thing Bob did not share with me was fear. Fear of accidents, injury, and death were overshadowed by the deep identity and meaning he derived from his work. There was nothing else he would rather do, in many ways, nothing else he could do. Bob was simply a fisher.

NOTES

INTRODUCTION

1. Jennifer M. Lincoln and Devin L. Lucas, "Occupational Fatalities in the United States Commercial Fishing Industry, 2000–2009," *Journal of Agromedicine* 15, no. 4 (2010): 343–350.

2. Mary E. Davis, "Occupational Safety and Regulatory Compliance in US Commercial Fishing," *Archives of Environmental and Occupational Health* 66, no. 4 (2011): 209–216.

3. US Department of Labor, Bureau of Labor Statistics, "National Census of Fatal Occupational Injuries in 2019," news release no. USDL-20-2265, December 16, 2020, https://www.bls.gov/news.release/archives/cfoi_12162020.pdf.

4. Michael G. Dyer, "Hazard and Risk in the New England Fishing Fleet," *Marine Technology* 37 (2000): 30–49; Di Jin and Eric Thunberg, "An Analysis of Fishing Vessel Accidents in Fishing Areas Off the Northeastern United States," *Safety Science* 43 (2005): 523–540.

5. Mary E. Davis, "Perceptions of Occupational Risk by US Commercial Fishermen," *Marine Policy* 36 (2012): 28–33.

6. John J. Poggie, Richard B. Pollnac, and S. Jones, "Perceptions of Vessel Safety Regulations: A Southern New England Fishery," *Marine Policy* 19 (1995): 411–418; Richard B. Pollnac, John J. Poggie, and Stephen L. Cabral, "Thresholds of Danger: Perceived Risk in a New England Fishery," *Human Organization* 57 (1998): 53–59; John J. Poggie, Richard B. Pollnac, and C. Van Dusen, "Intracultural Variability in the Cognition of Danger among Southern New England Fishers," *Marine Resource Economics* 11 (1996): 23–30; Ilene M. Kaplan and Hauke L. Kite-Powell, "Safety at Sea and Fisheries Management: Fishermen's Attitudes and the Need for Co-management," *Marine Policy* 24 (2000): 493–498.

7. Daniel Kahneman and Angus Deaton, "High Income Improves Evaluation of Life but Not Emotional Well-Being," *Proceedings of the National Academy of Sciences* 107, no. 38 (2010): 16489–16493.

8. Matthew A. Killingworth, Daniel Kahneman, and Barbara Mellers, "Income and Emotional Well-Being: A Conflict Resolved," *Proceedings of the National Academy of Sciences* 120, no. 1 (2023): e2208661120.

9. Robert Karasek and Tores Theorell, *Healthy Work: Stress, Productivity, and the Reconstruction of Working Life* (New York: Basic Books, 1990), 17.

10. Andrew Schwedel, James Root, James Allen, John Hazan, Eric Almquist, Thomas Devlin, and Karen Harris, *The Working Future: More Human, Not Less*, Bain and Company, 2022, https://www.bain.com/contentassets/d620202718c146359 acb05c02d9060db/bain-report_the-working-future.pdf.

11. US Department of Labor, Bureau of Labor Statistics, "Empirical Evidence for the 'Great Resignation,'" *Monthly Labor Review*, November 2022, https://doi .org/10.21916/mlr.2022.29.

12. Susan Lund, Anu Madgavkar, James Manyika, Sven Smit, Kweilin Ellingrud, Mary Meaney, and Olivia Robinson, *The Postpandemic Economy: The Future of Work after COVID-19*, McKinsey Global Institute, February 18, 2021, https://www .mckinsey.com/featured-insights/future-of-work/the-future-of-work-after-covid-19.

CHAPTER 1

1. Stephen Betts, "Captain Recounts Tragedy Off of Matinicus," *Bangor Daily News*, November 4, 2014, https://bangordailynews.com/2014/11/04/news/captain -recounts-tragedy-off-matinicus/.

2. Michael G. Dyer, "Hazard and Risk in the New England Fishing Fleet," *Marine Technology* 37 (2000): 30–49; Di Jin and Eric Thunberg, "An Analysis of Fishing Vessel Accidents in Fishing Areas Off the Northeastern United States," *Safety Science* 43 (2005): 523–540.

3. Mary E. Davis, "Occupational Safety and Regulatory Compliance in US Commercial Fishing," *Archives of Environmental and Occupational Health* 66, no. 4 (2011): 209–216.

4. Mary E. Davis, "Perceptions of Occupational Risk by US Commercial Fishermen," *Marine Policy* 36 (2012): 28–33.

5. National Research Council, National Academy of Sciences, *Fishing Vessel Safety: Blueprint for a National Program* (Washington, DC: National Academy Press, 1991); Lisa Pfeiffer, Tess Petesch, and Thamanna Vasan, "A Safer Catch? The Role of Fisheries Management in Fishing Safety," *Marine Resource Economics* 37, no. 1 (2022): 1–32; Anna M. Birkenback, David J. Kaczan, and Martin D. Smith, "Catch Shares Slow the Race to Fish," *Nature* 544 (2017): 223–226; Lisa Pfeiffer and Trevor Gratz, "The Effect of Rights-Based Fisheries Management on Risk Taking and Fishing Safety," *Proceedings of the National Academy of Sciences* 113, no. 10 (2016): 2615–2620.

6. Thomas DeLiere and Helen Levy, "Worker Sorting and the Risk of Death on the Job," *Journal of Labor Economics* 22, no. 4 (2004): 925–953.

7. Samuel Hill, "Maine Lobsterman Sentenced in Manslaughter Case," *National Fisherman*, March 21, 2019, https://www.nationalfisherman.com/national-inter national/maine-lobsterman-sentenced-manslaughter-case.

8. Angela W. Walter, Cesar Morocho, Lauren King, John Bartlett Jr., Debra Kelsey, Monica DeSousa, Gretchen Biesecker, and Laura Punnett, "Preventing Opioid Use Disorders among Fishing Industry Workers," *International Journal of Environmental Research and Public Health* 15, no. 648 (2018): 1–16.

9. Kevin E. Vowles, Mindy L. McEntee, Peter Siyahhan Julnes, Tessa Frohe, John P. Ney, and David N. van der Goes, "Rates of Opioid Misuse, Abuse, and Addiction in Chronic Pain: A Systematic Review and Data Synthesis," *Pain* 156 (2015): 569–576.

10. Massachusetts Department of Public Health, *Opioid-Related Overdose Deaths in Massachusetts by Industry and Occupation, 2011–2015*, August 2018, https://www .mass.gov/doc/opioid-related-overdose-deaths-in-massachusetts-by-industry -and-occupation-2011-2015/download.

11. Paul A. Schulte, Sudha Pandalai, Victoria Wulsin, and HeeKyoung Chun, "Interaction of Occupational and Personal Risk Factors in Workforce Health and Safety," *American Journal of Public Health* 102, no. 3 (2012): 434–448.

12. Mary E. Davis, Thomas J. Smith, Francine Laden, Jaime E. Hart, Andrew P. Blicharz, Paul Reaser, and Eric Garshick, "Driver Exposure to Combustion Particles in the US Trucking Industry," *Journal of Occupational and Environmental Hygiene* 4, no. 11 (2007): 848–854.

13. Jeff Brown, "Nearly 50 Years of Occupational Safety and Health Data," *Beyond the Numbers: Workplace Injurie* 9, no. 9 (2020), https://www.bls.gov/opub /btn/volume-9/pdf/nearly-50-years-of-occupational-safety-and-health-data.pdf.

14. US Department of Labor, Occupational Safety Health Administration, "Commonly Used Statistics," accessed May 23, 2023, https://www.osha.gov/data /commonstats.

15. Centers for Disease Control, National Institute for Occupational Safety and Health, *Fundamentals of Total Worker Health Approaches: Essential Elements for Advancing Worker Safety, Health, and Well-Being*, December 2016, https://www.cdc.gov /niosh/docs/2017-112/pdfs/2017_112.pdf.

16. Glorian Sorensen, Jack T. Dennerlein, Susan E. Peters, Erika L. Sabbath, Erin L. Kelly, and Gregory R. Wagner, "The Future of Research on Work, Safety, Health and Wellbeing: A Guiding Conceptual Framework," *Social Science and Medicine* 269 (2021): 113593; Susan E Peters, Jack T. Dennerlein, Gregory R. Wagner, and Glorian Sorensen, "Work and Worker Health in the Post-Pandemic World: A Public Health Perspective," *Lancet Public Health* 7 (2022): e188–e194.

17. World Health Organization, "Health and Care Worker Deaths during COVID," accessed May 23, 2023, https://www.who.int/news/item/20-10-2021 -health-and-care-worker-deaths-during-covid-19.

18. Marissa G. Baker, Trevor K. Peckham, and Noah S. Seixas, "Estimating the Burden of United States Workers Exposed to Infection or Disease: A Key Factor in Containing Risk of COVID-19 Infection," *PLOS One* 15, no. 4 (2020): e0232452.

19. Devan Hawkins, "Differential Occupational Risk for COVID-19 and Other Infection Exposure According to Race and Ethnicity," *American Journal of Industrial Medicine* 23145 (2020): 1–4.

20. Claire E. Hastie, David J. Lowe, Andrew McAuley, Andrew J. Winter, Nicholas L. Mills, Corri Black, Janet T. Scott, et al., "Outcomes among Confirmed Cases and a Matched Comparison Group in the Long-COVID in Scotland Study," *Nature Communications* 13, no. 5633 (2022): 1–9.

21. Andrew Schwedel, James Root, James Allen, John Hazan, Eric Almquist, Thomas Devlin, and Karen Harris, *The Working Future: More Human, Not Less*, Bain and Company, 2022, https://www.bain.com/contentassets/d620202718c146359 acb05c02d9060db/bain-report_the-working-future.pdf.

22. Centers for Disease Control and Prevention, National Institute for Occupational Safety and Health, *Commercial Fishing Fatality Summary: East Coast Region*, July 2017, https://www.cdc.gov/niosh/docs/2017-173/pdf/2017-173.pdf?id=10 .26616/NIOSHPUB2017173.

23. Alex Bryson, Richard Freeman, Claudio Lucifora, Michelle Pellizzari, and Virginie Pérotin, "Paying for Performance: Incentive Pay Schemes and Employees' Financial Participation," *Centre for Economic Performance*, no. 1112 (2012), http:// nrs.harvard.edu/urn-3:HUL.InstRepos:37146963.

24. Stephen A. McCurdy, Steven J. Samuels, Daniel J. Carroll, James J. Beaumont, and Lynne A. Morrin, "Agricultural Injury in California Migrant Hispanic Farm Workers," *American Journal of Industrial Medicine* 44 (2003): 225–235; Asim Saha, Takiar Ramnath, Ramendra N. Chaudhuri, and Habibullah N. Saiyed, "An Accident-Risk Assessment Study of Temporary Piece Rated Workers," *Industrial Health* 42 (2004): 240–245; Carin Sundstroem-Frisk, "Behavioral Control through Piece-Rate Wages," *Journal of Occupational Accidents* 6 (1984): 49–59; Keith A. Bender, Colin P. Green, and John S. Heywood, "Piece Rates and Workplace Injury: Does Survey Evidence Support Adam Smith?," *Journal of Population Economics* 25 (2012): 569–590; Benjamin Artz and John S. Heywood, "Performance Pay and Workplace Injury: Panel Evidence," *Economica* 82, no. suppl. 1 (2015): 1241–1260.

25. Keith A. Bender and Ionnis Theodossiou, "The Unintended Consequences of the Rat Race: The Detrimental Effects of Performance Pay on Health," *Oxford Economic Papers* 66 (2014): 824–847; Mary E. Davis, "Pay Matters: The Piece Rate

and Health in the Developing World," *Annals of Global Health* 82, no. 5 (2016): 858–865.

26. Arie Shirom, Mina Westman, and Samuel Melamed, "The Effects of Pay Systems on Blue Collar Employees' Emotional Distress: The Mediating Effects of Objective and Subjective Work Monotony," *Human Relations* 52 (1999): 1077–1097; Davis, "Pay Matters."

27. Michael S. Dahl and Lamar Pierce, "Pay-for-Performance and Employee Mental Health: Large Sample Evidence Using Employee Prescription Drug Usage," *Academy of Management Discoveries* 6, no. 1 (2020): 12–38.

28. Dominic Toupin, Luc Lebel, Denise Dubeau, Daniel Imbeau, and Luc Bouthillier, "Measuring the Productivity and Physical Workload of Brushcutters within the Context of a Production-Based Pay System," *Forest Policy Economics* 9 (2007): 1046–1055.

29. Bernd J. Frick, Ute Gotzen, and Robert Simmons, "The Hidden Costs of High-Performance Work Practices: Evidence from a Large German Steel Company," *Industrial and Labor Relations Review* 66 (2013): 189–214.

30. Mary E. Davis and Eric Hoyt, "A Longitudinal Study of Piece Rate and Health: Evidence and Implications for Workers in the Gig Economy," *Public Health* 180 (2020): 1–9; Edward P. Lazear, "Compensation and Incentives in the Workplace," *Journal of Economic Perspectives* 32, no. 3 (2018): 195–214.

31. Qianyao Pan, Daniel A. Sumner, Diane C. Mitchell, and Marc Schenker, "Compensation Incentives and Heat Exposure Affect Farm Worker Effort," *PLOS One* 16, no. 11 (2021): e0259459.

32. Edward P. Lazear, "Compensation and Incentives in the Workplace," *Journal of Economic Perspectives* 32, no. 3 (2018): 195–214.

33. Richard B. Freeman and Morris M. Kleiner, "The Last American Shoe Manufacturers: Changing the Method of Pay to Survive Foreign Competition," Working Paper No. 6750, National Bureau of Economic Research, 1998.

34. Mary E. Davis, "Piece Rate, Productivity, and Occupational Health in the Global Economy," International Labour Organization and Better Work, Discussion Paper No. 44, October 2021, https://betterwork.org/reports-and-publications/dp -44-piece-rate-productivity-and-occupational-health-in-the-global-economy/.

35. Davis, "Piece Rate, Productivity, and Occupational Health in the Global Economy."

36. US Department of Labor, Bureau of Labor Statistics, "Contingent and Alternative Work Employment Arrangements Summary," June 7, 2018, https://www .bls.gov/news.release/conemp.nr0.htm.

37. Lawrence F. Katz and Alan B. Krueger, "The Rise and Nature of Alternative Work Arrangements in the United States, 1995–2015," Working Paper No. 22667, National Bureau of Economic Research, 2016.

38. Lawrence F. Katz and Alan B. Krueger, "Understanding Trends in Alternative Work Arrangements in the United States," Working Paper No. 25425, National Bureau of Economic Research, 2019.

39. Pew Research Center, *The State of Gig Work in 2021* (Washington, DC: Pew Research Center, 2021), https://www.pewresearch.org/internet/2021/12/08/the-state-of-gig-work-in-2021/.

40. Juliet B. Schor, William Attwood-Charles, Mehmet Cansoy, Isak Ladegaard, and Robert Wengronowitz, "Dependence and Precarity in the Platform Economy," *Theory and Society* 49 (2020): 833–861.

41. Pew Research Center, *The State of Gig Work in 2021*.

42. Paul Glavin and Scott Schieman, "Dependency and Hardship in the Gig Economy: The Mental Health Consequences of Platform Work," *Socius: Sociological Research for a Dynamic World* 8 (2022): 1–13.

43. US Department of Labor, Bureau of Labor Statistics, "Median Earnings for Women in 2021 Were 83.1 Percent of the Median for Men," *Economics Daily*, January 24, 2022, https://www.bls.gov/opub/ted/2022/median-earnings-for-women-in-2021-were-83-1-percent-of-the-median-for-men.htm.

44. US Department of Labor, Bureau of Labor Statistics, *Women in the Labor Force: A Databook*, April 2021, https://www.bls.gov/opub/reports/womens-databook/2020/home.htm.

45. Peter Schnall, Marnie Dobson, Ellen Rosskam, and Ray Elling, *Unhealthy Work: Causes, Consequences, Cures* (London: Routledge, 2009).

46. Samuel B. Harvey, Matthew Modini, Sadhbh Joyce, Josie S. Milligan-Saville, Leona Tan, Arnstein Mykletun, Richard A. Bryant, Helen Christensen, and Philip B. Mitchell, "Can Work Make You Mentally Ill? A Systematic Meta-Review of Work-Related Risk Factors for Common Mental Health Problems," *Occupational and Environmental Medicine* 74 (2017): 301–310.

47. Robert A. Karasek, "Job Demands, Job Decision Latitude, and Mental Strain: Implications for Job Redesign," *Administrative Science Quarterly* 24 (1979): 285–308.

48. Jennifer L. Garza, Jacqueline M. Ferguson, Alicia G. Dugan, Ragan E Decker, Rick A. Laguerre, Adekemi O. Suleiman, and Jennifer M. Cavallari, "Investigating the Relationship between Working Time Characteristics on Musculoskeletal Symptoms: A Cross Sectional Study," *Archives of Environmental and Occupational Health* 18 (2020): 1–8.

49. L. Ala-Mursula, J. Vahtera, J. Pentti, and M. Kivimaki, "Effect of Employee Worktime Control on Health: A Prospective Cohort Study," *Occupational and Environmental Medicine* 61 (2004): 254–261.

50. Hylco H. Nijp, Debby G. Beckers, Sabine A. Geurts, Philip Tucker, and Michiel A. Kompier, "Systematic Review on the Association between Employee

Worktime Control and Work–Non-Work Balance, Health and Well-Being, and Job-Related Outcomes," *Scandinavian Journal of Work Environment and Health* 38, no. 4 (2012): 299–313.

51. Meg Lovejoy, Erin L. Kelly, Laura D. Kubzansky, and Lisa F. Berkman, "Work Redesign for the 21st Century: Promising Strategies for Enhancing Worker Well-Being," *American Journal of Public Health* 111, no. 10 (2021): 1787–1795.

52. Goran Kecklund and John Axelsson, "Health Consequences of Shift Work and Insufficient Sleep," *BMJ* 355 (2016): i5210.

53. Adovich S. Rivera, Maxwell Akanbi, Linda C. O'Dwyer, and Megan McHugh, "Shift Work and Long Hours and Their Association with Chronic Health Conditions: A Systematic Review of Systematic Reviews with Meta-Analyses," *PLOS One* 15, no. 4 (2020): e0231037.

54. International Agency for Research on Cancer, "Carcinogenicity of Night Shift Work," *The Lancet Oncology* 20 (2019): 1058–1059.

55. Jacqui Wise, "Danish Night Shift Workers with Breast Cancer Awarded Compensation," *BMJ* 338 (2009): b1152.

56. Nina Vujović, Matthew J. Piron, Jingyi Qian, Sarah L. Chellappa, Arlet Nedeltcheva, David Barr, Su W. Heng, et al., "Late Isocaloric Eating Increases Hunger, Decreases Energy Expenditure, and Modifies Metabolic Pathways in Adults with Overweight and Obesity," *Cell Metabolism* 34 (2022): 1486–1498.

57. Goran Kecklund and John Axelsson, "Health Consequences of Shift Work and Insufficient Sleep," *BMJ* 355 (2016): i5210.

58. Mary E. Davis, "Health Effects of Night and Irregular Shiftwork: A Longitudinal Cohort Study of US Workers," *Journal of Occupational and Environmental Medicine* 63, no. 4 (2021): 265–269.

59. Yixuan Zhao, Alice Richardson, Carmel Poyser, Peter Butterworth, Lindall Strazdins, and Liana S. Leach, "Shift Work and Mental Health: A Systematic Review and Meta-Analysis," *International Archives of Occupational and Environmental Health* 92 (2019): 763–793.

60. Daniel Schneider and Kristen Harknett, "Consequences of Routine Work-Schedule Instability for Worker Health and Well-Being," *American Sociological Review* 84, no. 1 (2019): 82–114.

61. Joshua Choper, Daniel Schneider, and Kristen Harknett, "Uncertain Time: Precarious Schedules and Job Turnover in the US Service Sector," *ILR Review* 75, no. 5 (2022): 1099–1132.

62. Kristen Harknett, Daniel Scneider, and Irwin Veronique, "Improving Health and Economic Security by Reducing Work Schedule Uncertainty," *Proceedings of the National Academy of Sciences* 118, no. 42 (2021): e2107828118.

63. Julia R. Henly and Susan J. Lambert, "Unpredictable Work Timing in Retail Jobs: Implications for Employee Work-Life Conflict," *Industrial and Labor Relations Review* 67 (2014): 986–1016.

64. Robert Tuttle and Michael Garr, "Shift Work and Work to Family Fit: Does Schedule Control Matter?," *Journal of Family and Economic Issues* 33 (2012): 261–271; Sigrid Luhr, Daniel Schneider, and Kristen Harknett, "Parenting without Predictability: Precarious Schedules, Parental Strain, and Work-Life Conflict," *The Russell Sage Foundation Journal of the Social Sciences* 8, no. 5 (2022): 24–44.

65. Leah R. Abrams, Kristen Harknett, and Daniel Schneider, "Older Workers with Unpredictable Schedules: Implications for Well-Being and Job Retention," *The Gerontologist* 62, no. 10 (2022): 1443–1453.

66. Susan J. Lambert, Anna Haley-Lock, and Julia R. Henly, "Schedule Flexibility in Hourly Jobs: Unanticipated Consequences and Promising Directions," *Community, Work and Family* 15, no. 3 (2012): 293–315.

67. Joan C. Williams, Susan J. Lambert, Saravanan Kesavan, Peter J. Fugiel, Lori A. Ospina, Erin D. Rapoport, Meghan Jarpe, et al., *Stable Scheduling Increases Productivity and Sales: The Stable Scheduling Study*, 2018, https://worklifelaw.org/publications/Stable-Scheduling-Study-Report.pdf.

68. Williams et al., *Stable Scheduling Study*.

69. US Census Bureau, "The Number of People Primarily Working from Home Tripled between 2019 and 2021," September 15, 2022, https://www.census.gov/newsroom/press-releases/2022/people-working-from-home.html.

70. Jonathan I. Dingel and Brent Neiman, "How Many Jobs Can Be Done at Home?," *Journal of Public Economics* 189 (2020): 104235.

71. Susan Lund, Anu Madgavkar, James Manyika, Sven Smit, Kweilin Ellingrud, Mary Meaney, and Olivia Robinson, *The Postpandemic Economy: The Future of Work after COVID-19*, McKinsey Global Institute, February 18, 2021, https://www.mckinsey.com/featured-insights/future-of-work/the-future-of-work-after-covid-19.

72. Tammy D. Allen, Timothy D. Golden, and Kristen M. Shockley, "How Effective Is Telecommuting? Assessing the Status of Our Scientific Findings," *Psychological Science in the Public Interest* 16, no. 2 (2015): 40–68.

73. Prithwiraj Choudhury, Tarun Khanna, Christos A. Makridis, and Kyle Schirmann, "Is Hybrid Work the Best of Both Worlds? Evidence from a Field Experiment," Working Paper No. 22-063, Harvard Business School, March 2022.

74. Duanyi Yang, Erin L. Kelly, Laura D. Kubzansky, and Lisa Berkman, "Working from Home and Worker Well-Being: New Evidence from Germany," *ILR Review* 76, no. 3 (2023): 504–531.

75. Evan DeFilippis, Stephen M. Impink, Madison Singell, Jeff Polzer, and Raffaella Sadun, "The Impact of COVID-19 on Digital Communication Patterns," *Humanities and Social Sciences Communications* 9, no. 180 (2022): 1–11.

76. Lonqi Yang, David Holtz, Sonia Jaffe, Siddharth Suri, Shilpi Sinha, Jeffrey Weston, Connor Joyce, et al., "The Effects of Remote Work on Collaboration among Information Workers," *Nature Human Behaviour* 6 (2022): 43–54.

77. Melanie S. Brucks and Jonathan Levav, "Virtual Communication Curbs Creative Idea Generation," *Nature* 615 (2022): 108–112.

78. Dingel and Neiman, "How Many Jobs Can Be Done at Home?"

79. Jose M. Barrero, Nicholas Bloom, and Steven J. Davis, "Why Working from Home Will Stick," Working Paper No. 28731, National Bureau of Economic Research, 2021.

80. Lund et al., *The Postpandemic Economy*.

81. Lebene R. Soga, Yemisi Bolade-Ogunfodun, Marcello Mariani, Rita Nasr, Benjamin Laker, "Unmasking the Other Face of Flexible Working Practices: A Systematic Literature Review," *Journal of Business Research* 142 (2022): 648–662.

CHAPTER 2

1. Deborah D. Danner, David A. Snowdon, and Wallace V. Friesen, "Positive Emotions in Early Life and Longevity: Findings from the Nun Study," *Journal of Personality and Social Psychology* 80, no. 5 (2001): 804–813.

2. Danner, Snowdon, and Friesen, "Positive Emotions in Early Life and Longevity," 806.

3. Danner, Snowdon, and Friesen, 806.

4. David A. Snowdon, "Aging and Alzheimer's Disease: Lessons from the Nun Study," *Gerontologist* 37 (1997): 150–156.

5. Laura B. Shrestha, "Life Expectancy in the United States," Congressional Research Service Document 7-5700 (2006).

6. Ed Diener, Shigehiro Oishi, and Louis Tay, "Advances in Subjective Well-Being Research," *Nature Human Behaviour* 2 (2018): 253–260.

7. Aysu Okbay, Bart M. Baselmans, Jan-Emamanuel De Neve, Patrick Turley, Michel G. Nivard, Mark A. Fontana, S. Fleur Meddens, et al., "Genetic Variants Associated with Subjective Well-Being, Depressive Symptoms, and Neuroticism Identified through Genome-Wide Analyses," *Nature Genetics* 48, no. 6 (2015): 624–638.

8. Andrew Steptoe, Angus Deaton, and Arthur A. Stone, "Subjective Wellbeing, Health, and Ageing," *Lancet* 385 (2015): 640–648.

9. Andrew Steptoe, "Happiness and Health," *Annual Review of Public Health* 40 (2019): 339–359.

10. Michael E. Sadler, Christopher J. Miller, Kaare Christensen, and Matt McGue, "Subjective Well-Being and Longevity: A Cotwin Control Study," *Twin Research and Human Genetics* 14, no. 3 (2011): 249–256.

11. Dan Ariely, *Predictably Irrational: The Hidden Forces That Shape Our Decisions* (New York: Harper Collins, 2008).

12. Hakan Eggert and Peter Martinsson, "Are Commercial Fishers Risk-Lovers?," *Land Economics* 80 (2004): 550–560.

13. John J. Poggie, Richard B. Pollnac, and S. Jones, "Perceptions of Vessel Safety Regulations: A Southern New England Fishery," *Marine Policy* 19 (1995): 411–418; Richard B. Pollnac, John J. Poggie, and Stephen L. Cabral, "Thresholds of Danger: Perceived Risk in a New England Fishery," *Human Organization* 57 (1998): 53–59.

14. Mary E. Davis, "Perceptions of Occupational Risk by US Commercial Fishermen," *Marine Policy* 36 (2012): 28–33.

15. Poggie, Pollnac, and Jones, "Perceptions of Vessel Safety Regulations"; Pollnac, Poggie, and Cabral, "Thresholds of Danger."

16. Mary A. McDonald and Kristen L. Kucera, "Understanding Non-Industrialized Workers' Approaches to Safety: How Do Commercial Fishermen 'Stay Safe'?," *Journal of Safety Research* 38 (2007): 289–297.

17. Richard Easterlin, "Does Economic Growth Improve the Human Lot? Some Empirical Evidence," in *Nations and Households in Economic Growth*, ed. Paul A. David and Melvin W. Reder (New York: Academic Press, 1974).

18. Carol Graham, *Happiness around the World: The Paradox of Happy Peasants and Miserable Millionaires* (New York: Oxford University Press, 2010); Diener, Oishi, and Tay, "Advances in Subjective Well-Being Research."

19. Daniel Kahneman and Angus Deaton, "High Income Improves Evaluation of Life but Not Emotional Well-Being," *Proceedings of the National Academy of Sciences* 107, no. 38 (2010): 16489–16493.

20. Matthew A. Killingsworth, "Experienced Well-Being Rises with Income, Even Above $75,000 per Year," *Proceedings of the National Academy of Sciences* 118, no. 4 (2020): e2016976118.

21. Matthew A. Killingworth, Daniel Kahneman, and Barbara Mellers, "Income and Emotional Well-Being: A Conflict Resolved," *Proceedings of the National Academy of Sciences* 120, no. 1 (2023): e2208661120.

22. Andrew T. Jebb, Louis Tay, Ed Diener, and Shigehiro Oishi, "Happiness, Income Satiation, and Turning Points around the World," *Nature Human Behaviour* 2 (2018): 33–38.

23. Carol Graham and Eduardo Lora, *Paradox and Perception: Measuring Quality of Life in Latin America* (Washington DC: Brookings Institution Press, 2009).

24. Graham, *Happiness around the World*.

25. Richard Layard, *Happiness: Lessons from a New Science* (New York: Penguin Press, 2005), 48.

26. Graham, *Happiness around the World*.

27. Layard, *Happiness: Lessons from a New Science*.

28. Erzo F. Luttmer, "Neighbors as Negatives: Relative Earnings and Well-Being," *Quarterly Journal of Economics* 120, no. 3 (2005): 963–1002.

29. Richard B. Freeman, "Job Satisfaction as an Economic Variable," Working Paper No. 0225, National Bureau of Economic Research, 1977; George J. Borjas, "Job Satisfaction, Wages, and Unions," *Journal of Human Resources* 14, no. 1 (1979): 21–40.

30. Eleonora Topino, Annamaria Di Fabio, Letizia Palazzeschi, and Alessio Gori, "Personality Traits, Worker's Age, and Job Satisfaction: The Moderated Effect of Conscientiousness," *PLOS One* 16, no. 7 (2021): e0252275.

31. David G. Blanchflower, Alex Bryson, and Colin Green, "Trade Unions and the Well-Being of Workers," *British Journal of Industrial Relations* 60 (2022): 255–277.

32. Shani Pindek, Zhiqing E. Zhou, Stacey R. Kessler, Alexandra Krajcevska, and Paul E. Spector, "Workdays Are Not Created Equal: Job Satisfaction and Job Stressors across the Workweek," *Human Relations* 74, no. 9 (2021): 1447–1472.

33. Matthias Benz and Bruno S. Frey, "Being Independent Is a Great Thing: Subjective Evaluations of Self-Employment and Hierarchy," *Economica* 75 (2008): 362–383.

34. Brian Faragher, Monica Cass, and Cary Cooper, "The Relationship between Job Satisfaction and Health: A Meta-Analysis," *Occupational and Environmental Medicine* 62 (2005): 105–112.

35. Faragher, Cass, and Cooper, "The Relationship between Job Satisfaction and Health: A Meta-Analysis."

36. Jo Phelan, "The Paradox of the Contented Female Worker: An Assessment of Alternative Explanations," *Social Psychology Quarterly* 57, no. 2 (1994): 95–107.

37. US Department of Labor, Bureau of Labor Statistics, "Median Earnings for Women in 2021 Were 83.1 Percent of the Median for Men," *Economics Daily*, January 24, 2022, https://www.bls.gov/opub/ted/2022/median-earnings-for-women-in-2021-were-83-1-percent-of-the-median-for-men.htm.

38. Shoshana R. Dobrow, Yoav Ganzach, and Yihao Liu, "Time and Job Satisfaction: A Longitudinal Study of the Differential Roles of Age and Tenure," *Journal of Management* 44, no. 7 (2016): 2558–2579.

39. Conchita D'Ambrosio, Andrew E. Clark, and Marta Barazzetta, "Unfairness at Work: Well-Being and Quits," *Labour Economics* 51 (2018): 307–316.

40. Shakked Noy and Isabelle Sin, "The Effects of Neighbourhood and Workplace Income Comparisons on Subjective Well-Being," *Journal of Economic Behavior and Organization* 185 (2021): 918–945.

41. Matthias Collischon, "Relative Pay, Rank, and Happiness: A Comparison between Genders and Part- and Full-Time Employees," *Journal of Happiness Studies* 20 (2019): 67–80.

42. D'Ambrosio, Clark, and Barazzetta, "Unfairness at Work: Well-Being and Quits."

43. David Card, Alexandre Mas, Enrico Moretti, and Emmanuel Saez, "Inequality at Work: The Effect of Peer Salaries on Job Satisfaction," *American Economic Review* 102, no. 6 (2012): 2981–3003.

44. Justin M. Berg, Amy Wresniewski, Adam M. Grant, Jennifer Kurkoski, and Brian Welle, "Getting Unstuck: The Effects of Growth Mindsets About the Self and Job on Happiness at Work," *Journal of Applied Psychology* 108, no. 1 (2003): 152–166.

CHAPTER 3

1. International Agency for Research on Cancer, "Press Release 213: Diesel Exhaust Carcinogenic," June 12, 2012, https://www.iarc.who.int/wp-content/uploads/2018/07/pr213_E.pdf.

2. Christopher J. Ruhm, "Are Recessions Good for Your Health?," *Quarterly Journal of Economics* 115 (2000): 617–650.

3. Katharina Janke, Kevin Lee, Carol Propper, Kalvinder Shields, and Michael A. Shields, "Macroeconomic Conditions and Health in Britain: Aggregation, Dynamics and Local Area Heterogeneity," Discussion Paper Series 13091, IZA Institute of Labor Economics, 2020; Jason M. Lindo, "Aggregation and the Estimated Effects of Economic Conditions on Health," *Journal of Health Economics* 40 (2015): 83–96.

4. Janke, Kevin Lee, Carol Propper, Kalvinder Shields, and Michael A. Shields, "Macroeconomic Conditions and Health in Britain."

5. Erdal Tekin, Chandler McClellan, and Karen J. Minyard, "Health and Health Behaviors during the Worst of Times: Evidence from the Great Recession," Discussion Paper Series 7538, IZA Institute of Labor Economics, 2013.

6. Anne Case and Angus Deaton, "Rising Morbidity and Mortality in Midlife among White Non-Hispanic Americans in the 21st Century," *Proceedings of the National Academy of Sciences* 112, no. 49 (2015): 15078–15083.

7. Case and Deaton, "Rising Morbidity and Mortality in Midlife among White Non-Hispanic Americans."

8. Massachusetts Department of Public Health, *Opioid-Related Overdose Deaths in Massachusetts by Industry and Occupation, 2011–2015*, August 2018, https://www.mass.gov/doc/opioid-related-overdose-deaths-in-massachusetts-by-industry-and-occupation-2011-2015/download.

9. Robert DeFina and Lance Hannon, "De-unionization and Drug Death Rates," *Social Currents* 6, no. 1 (2019): 4–13.

10. Peter Schnall, Marnie Dobson, Ellen Rosskam, and Ray Elling. *Unhealthy Work: Causes, Consequences, Cures* (London: Routledge, 2009).

11. Eileen Y. Chou, Bidhan L. Parmar, and Adam D. Galinsky, "Economic Insecurity Increases Physical Pain," *Psychological Science* 27, no. 4 (2016): 443–454.

12. Sepideh Modrek and Mark R. Cullen, "Job Insecurity during Recessions: Effects on Survivors' Work Stress," *BMC Public Health* 13, no. 929 (2013): 1–11.

13. Mary E. Davis, "Recessions and Health: The Impact of Economic Trends on Air Pollution in California," *American Journal of Public Health* 102, no. 10 (2012): 1951–1956.

14. Mary E. Davis, Francine Laden, Jaime E. Hart, Eric Garshick, and Thomas J. Smith, "Economic Activity and Ambient Air Pollution Trends," *Environmental Health Perspectives* 118, no. 5 (2010): 614–619.

15. James Hall, Ilias Goranitis, Jesse Kigozi, and Allesandra Guariglia, "New Evidence on the Impact of the Great Recession on Health-Compromising Behaviors," *Economics and Human Biology* 41 (2021): 1–9; Xavier Bartroll, Veronica Toffolutti, Davide Malmusi, Laia Palencia, Carme Borrell, and Marc Suhrcke, "Health and Health Behaviours before and during the Great Recession, Overall and by Socioeconomic Status, Using Data from Four Repeated Cross-Sectional Health Surveys in Spain (2001–2012)," *BMC Public Health* 15, no. 865 (2015): 1–12; Marina Bosque-Prous, Anton E. Kunst, M. Teresa Brugal, and Albert Espelt, "Changes in Alcohol Consumption in the 50- to 64-Year-Old European Economically Active Population during an Economic Crisis," *European Journal of Public Health* 27, no. 4 (2017): 711–716.

16. Christopher J. Ruhm, "Healthy Living in Hard Times," *Journal of Health Economics* 24, no. 2 (2005): 341–363; Gregory Coleman and Dhaval Dave, "Exercise, Physical Activity, and Exertion over the Business Cycle," *Social Science and Medicine* 93 (2013): 11–20.

17. Kristian Wahlbeck and David McDaid, "Actions to Alleviate the Mental Health Impact of the Economic Crisis," *World Psychiatry* 11 (2012): 139–145; Melissa McInerney, Jennifer M. Mellor, and Lauren H. Nicholas, "Recession Depression: Mental Health Effects of the 2008 Stock Market Crash," *Journal of Health Economics* 32, no. 6 (2013): 1090–1104.

18. Michael O. Harhay, Jacob Bor, Sanjay Basu, Martin McKee, Jennifer S. Mindell, Nicola J. Shelton, and David Stuckler, "Differential Impact of the Economic Recession on Alcohol Use among White British Adults, 2004–2010," *European Journal of Public Health* 24, no. 3 (2013): 410–415.

19. Mireia Jofre-Bonet, Victoria Serra-Sastre, and Sotiris Vandoros, "The Impact of the Great Recession on Health-Related Risk Factors, Behaviour, and Outcomes in England," *Social Science and Medicine* 197 (2018): 213–225.

20. Ed Diener, Shigehiro Oishi, and Louis Tay, "Advances in Subjective Well-Being Research," *Nature Human Behaviour* 2 (2018): 253–260.

21. Maike Luhman, Wilhelm Hofmann, Michael Eid, and Richard E. Lucas, "Subjective Well-Being and Adaptation to Life Events: A Meta-Analysis," *Journal of Personality and Social Psychology* 102, no. 3 (2012): 592–615.

22. Eunkook M. Suh, Ed Diener, and Frank Fujita, "Events and Subjective Well-Being: Only Recent Events Matter," *Journal of Personality and Social Psychology* 5 (1996): 1091–1102.

23. Rainer Winklemann, "Unemployment and Happiness," IZA World of Labor, October 2014, https://wol.iza.org/uploads/articles/94/pdfs/unemployment-and-happiness.pdf.

24. Petri Bockerman and Pekka Ilmakunnas, "Elusive Effects of Unemployment on Happiness," *Social Indicators Research* 79 (2006): 159–169; Petri Bockerman and Pekka Ilmakunnas, "Unemployment and Self-Assessed Health: Evidence from Panel Data," *Health Economics* 18 (2009): 161–179.

25. Dora Gudmundsdottir, "The Impact of Economic Crises on Happiness," *Social Indicators Research* 110 (2013): 1083–1101.

26. Amos Tversky and Daniel Kahneman, "Judgement under Uncertainty: Heuristics and Biases: Biases in Judgments Reveal Some Heuristics of Thinking under Uncertainty," *Science* 185, no. 4157 (1974): 1124–1131.

27. Daniela D. Avila and Kurt G. Lunsford, "Underemployment Following the Great Recession and the COVID Recession," Economic Commentary, Federal Reserve Bank of Cleveland 2022-01, February 3, 2022, https://doi.org/10.26509/frbc-ec-202201.

28. David N. Bell and David G. Blanchflower, "Underemployment in the United States and Europe," *ILR Review* 74, no. 1 (2021): 56–94.

29. David N. Bell and David G. Blanchflower, "The Well-Being of the Overemployed and the Underemployed and the Rise in Depression in the UK," *Journal of Economic Behavior and Organization* 161 (2019): 180–196.

30. Milena Nikolova and Carol Graham, "Employment, Late-Life Work, Retirement, and Well-Being in Europe and the United States," *IZA Journal of European Labor Studies* 3, no. 5 (2014): 1–30.

31. Federal Reserve Bank of St. Louis, "Self-Employment Grows during COVID-19 Pandemic," July 5, 2022, https://www.stlouisfed.org/on-the-economy /2022/jul/self-employment-returns-growth-path-pandemic.

32. Barton H. Hamilton, "Does Entrepreneurship Pay? An Empirical Analysis of the Returns to Self-Employment," *Journal of Political Economy* 108, no. 3 (2000): 604–631.

33. Ross Levine and Yona Rubinstein, "Smart and Illicit: Who Becomes an Entrepreneur and Do They Earn More?," *Quarterly Journal of Economics* 132, no. 2 (2017): 963–1018.

34. Matthias Benz and Bruno S. Frey, "Being Independent Is a Great Thing: Subjective Evaluations of Self-Employment and Hierarchy," Economica 75 (2008): 362–383; Matthias Benz and Bruno S. Frey, "The Value of Doing What You Like: Evidence from the Self-Employed in 23 Countries," *Journal of Economic Behavior and Organization* 68 (2008): 445–455; David G. Blanchflower, "Self-Employment in OECD Countries," *Labour Economics* 7 (2000): 471–505.

35. Martin Binder and Alexander Coad, "Life Satisfaction and Self-Employment: A Matching Approach," *Small Business Economics* 40, no. 4 (2013): 1009–1033; Jessie Gevaert, Karen Van Aerden, Deborah De Moortel, and Christophe Vanroelen, "Employment Quality as a Health Determinant: Empirical Evidence for the Waged and Self-Employed," *Work and Occupations* 48, no. 2 (2021): 146–183; Johan P. Larsson and Per Thulin, "Independent by Necessity? The Life Satisfaction of Necessity and Opportunity Entrepreneurs in 70 Countries," *Small Business Economics* 53, no. 4 (2019): 921–934; Maria Abreu, Ozge Oner, Aleid Brouwer, and Eveline van Leeuwen, "Well-Being Effects of Self-Employment: A Spatial Inquiry," *Entrepreneurship and Wellbeing* 34, no. 4 (2019): 589–607.

36. Nikolova and Graham, "Employment, Late-Life Work, Retirement, and Well-Being."

37. Abreu et al., "Well-Being Effects of Self-Employment."

38. Seth A. Berkowitz, Rachel Gold, Marisa Elena Domino, and Sanjay Basu, "Health Insurance Coverage and Self-Employment," *Health Services Research* 56, no. 2 (2021): 247–255.

39. Jangho Yoon and Stephanie L. Bernell, "The Effect of Self-Employment on Health, Access to Care, and Health Behavior," *Health* 5, no. 12 (2013): 2116–2127.

40. George J. Borjas, "Job Satisfaction, Wages, and Unions," *Journal of Human Resources* 14, no. 1 (1979): 21–40.

41. Alex Bryson and Michael White, "Not So Dissatisfied After All? The Impact of Union Coverage on Job Satisfaction," *Oxford Economic Papers* 68, no. 4 (2016): 898–919.

42. David G. Blanchflower, Alex Bryson, and Colin Green, "Trade Unions and the Well-Being of Workers," *British Journal of Industrial Relations* 60 (2022): 255–277.

43. Henry S. Farber, Daniel Herbst, Ilyana Kuziemko, and Suresh Naidu, "Unions and Inequality of the Twentieth Century: New Evidence from Survey Data," *Quarterly Journal of Economics* 136, no. 3 (2021): 1325–1385.

44. J. Paul Leigh and Bozhidar Chakalov, "Labor Unions and Health: A Literature Review of Pathways and Outcomes in the Workplace," *Preventative Medicine Reports* 24 (2021): 1–10.

45. Jerzy Eisenberg-Guyot, Stephen J. Mooney, Wendy E. Barrington, and Anjum Hajat, "Does the Union Make Us Strong? Labor-Union Membership, Self-Rated Health, and Mental Illness: A Parametric G-Formula Approach," *American Journal of Epidemiology* 190, no. 4 (2020): 630–641.

46. Alejandro Donado and Klaus Walde, "How Trade Unions Increase Welfare," *The Economic Journal* 122 (2012): 990–1009.

47. US Department of Labor, Bureau of Labor Statistics, "Union Members Summary," *Economic News Release*, January 19, 2023, https://www.bls.gov/news .release/union2.nr0.htm.

48. US Department of Labor, Bureau of Labor Statistics, "Union Membership in the United States," *Spotlight on Statistics*, September 2016, https://www.bls.gov /spotlight/2016/union-membership-in-the-united-states/pdf/union-membership -in-the-united-states.pdf.

49. National Labor Relations Board, "First Three Quarters' Union Election Petitions up 56%, Exceeding All FY21 Petitions Filed," July 13, 2022, https://www .nlrb.gov/news-outreach/news-story/first-three-quarters-union-election-petitions -up-56-exceeding-all-fy21.

50. Zander S. Venter, Kristin Aunan, Sourangsu Chowdhury, and Jos Lelieveld, "COVID-19 Lockdowns Cause Global Air Pollution Declines," *Proceedings of the National Academy of Sciences* 117, no. 32 (2020): 18984–18990.

51. Susan Lund, Anu Madgavkar, James Manyika, Sven Smit, Kweilin Ellingrud, Mary Meaney, and Olivia Robinson, *The Postpandemic Economy: The Future of Work after COVID-19*, McKinsey Global Institute, February 18, 2021, https://www .mckinsey.com/featured-insights/future-of-work/the-future-of-work-after -covid-19.

52. Ian Cook, "Who Is Driving the Great Resignation?," *Harvard Business Review*, September 15, 2021, https://hbr.org/2021/09/who-is-driving-the-great-resignation.

CHAPTER 4

1. Aristotle, *Nicomachean Ethics*, trans. Hugh T. Thomson (London: Penguin Books, 2004).

2. Andrew Steptoe, "Happiness and Health," *Annual Review of Public Health* 40 (2019): 339–359.

3. Viktor Frankl, *Man's Search for Meaning* (Boston: Beacon Press, 1959), 67.

4. Patricia A. Boyle, Aron S. Buchman, Lisa L. Barnes, and David A. Bennett, "Effect of a Purpose in Life on Risk of Incident Alzheimer Disease and Mild Cognitive Impairment in Community-Dwelling Older Persons," *Archives of General Psychiatry* 67, no. 3 (2010): 304–310.

5. Patricia A. Boyle, Aron S. Buchman, and David A. Bennet D, "Purpose in Life is Associated with a Reduced Risk of Incident Disability among Community-Dwelling Older Persons," *American Journal of Geriatric Psychiatry* 18, no. 12 (2010): 1093–1102.

6. Eric S. Kim, Jennifer K. Sun, Nansook Park, and Christopher Peterson, "Purpose in Life and Reduced Incidence of Stroke in Older Adults: 'The Health and Retirement Study,'" *Journal of Psychosomatic Research* 74 (2013): 427–432.

7. Eric S. Kim, Ichiro Kawachi, Ying Chen, Laura D. Kubzansky, "Association between Purpose in Life and Objective Measures of Physical Function in Older Adults," *JAMA Psychiatry* 74, no. 10 (2017): 1039–1045.

8. Judith A. Okely, Cyrus Cooper, and Catharine R. Gale, "Wellbeing and Arthritis Incidence: The Survey of Health, Ageing and Retirement in Europe," *Annals of Behavioral Medicine* 50 (2016): 419–426.

9. Patrick L. Hill and Nicholas A. Turiano, "Purpose in Life as a Predictor of Mortality across Adulthood," *Psychological Science* 25, no. 7 (2014): 1482–146; Andrew Steptoe, Angus Deaton, and Arthur A. Stone, "Subjective Wellbeing, Health, and Ageing," *Lancet* 385 (2015): 640–648; Paola Zaninotto, Jane Wardle, and Andrew Steptoe, "Sustained Enjoyment of Life and Mortality at Older Ages: Analysis of the English Longitudinal Study of Ageing," *BMJ* 355 (2016): i6267.

10. Eric S. Kim, Victor J. Strecher, and Carol D. Ryff, "Purpose in Life and Use of Preventative Health Care Services," *Proceedings of the National Academy of Sciences* 111, no. 46 (2014): 16331–16336.

11. William A. Kahn, "Psychological Conditions of Personal Engagement and Disengagement at Work," *The Academy of Management Journal* 33, no. 4 (1990): 692–724.

12. Catherine Bailey, Ruth Yeoman, Adrian Madden, Marc Thompson, and Gary Kerridge, "A Review of the Empirical Literature on Meaningful Work: Progress and Research Agenda," *Human Resource Development Review* 18, no. 1 (2019): 83–113.

13. Abraham H. Maslow, *Motivation and Personality* (New York: Harper and Row, 1954).

14. David A. Snowdon, "Aging and Alzheimer's Disease: Lessons from the Nun Study," *Gerontologist* 37 (1997): 150–156.

15. Margaret M. McGuinness, *Called to Serve: A History of Nuns in America* (New York: New York University Press, 2013).

16. Franciscan Children's, "Our History," accessed May 23, 2023, https://francis canchildrens.org/about/our-history/.

17. McGuinness, *Called to Serve: A History of Nuns in America*.

18. McGuinness, *Called to Serve: A History of Nuns in America*.

19. Laura B. Shrestha, "Life Expectancy in the United States," Congressional Research Service Document 7-5700 (2006).

20. Deborah D. Danner, David A. Snowdon, and Wallace V. Friesen, "Positive Emotions in Early Life and Longevity: Findings from the Nun Study," *Journal of Personality and Social Psychology* 80, no. 5 (2001): 804–13.

21. Center for Applied Research in the Apostolate, "Frequently Requested Church Statistics," accessed May 23, 2023, https://cara.georgetown.edu/faqs.

22. McGuinness, *Called to Serve: A History of Nuns in America*.

23. Brent D. Rosso, Kathryn H. Dekas, and Amy Wrzesniewski, "On the Meaning of Work: A Theoretical Integration and Review," *Research in Organizational Behavior* 30 (2010): 91–127.

24. Marjolein Lips-Wiersma and Sarah Wright, "Measuring the Meaning of Meaningful Work: Development and Validation of the Comprehensive Meaningful Work Scale (CMWS)," *Group and Organization Management* 37, no. 5 (2012): 655–685.

25. Bailey et al., "A Review of the Empirical Literature on Meaningful Work."

26. Catherine Bailey, Adrian Madden, Kerstin Alfes, Amanda Shantz, and Emma Soane, "The Mismanaged Soul: Existential Labor and the Erosion of Meaningful Work," *Human Resource Management Review* 27 (2017): 416–430.

27. Mariolein Lips-Wiersma, Sarah Wright, and Bryan Dik, "Meaningful Work: Differences among Blue-, Pink-, and White-Collar Occupations," *Career Development International* 21, no. 5 (2016): 534–551.

28. Catherine Bailey and Adrian Madden, "What Makes Work Meaningful—Or Meaningless," *MIT Sloan Management Review* 57, no. 4 (2016): 53–61.

29. Douglas R. May, Richard L. Gilson, and Lynn M. Harter, "The Psychological Conditions of Meaningfulness, Safety, and Availability and the Engagement of the Human Spirit at Work," *Journal of Occupational and Organizational Psychology* 77 (2004): 11–37.

30. Bailey et al., "The Mismanaged Soul."

31. David Graeber, *Bullshit Jobs: A Theory* (New York: Simon and Schuster, 2019).

32. Andrew Schwedel, James Root, James Allen, John Hazan, Eric Almquist, Thomas Devlin, and Karen Harris, *The Working Future: More Human, Not Less*, Bain and Company, 2022, https://www.bain.com/contentassets/d620202718 c146359acb05c02d9060db/bain-report_the-working-future.pdf.

33. Catherine Bailey and Adrian Madden, "Time Reclaimed: Temporality and the Experience of Meaningful Work," *Work, Employment, and Society* 31, no. 1 (2017): 3–18.

34. Gretchen Berlin, Meredith Lapointe, and Mhoire Murphy, "Surveyed Nurses Consider Leaving Direct Patient Care at Elevated Rates," McKinsey and Company, February 17, 2022, https://www.mckinsey.com/industries/healthcare -systems-and-services/our-insights/surveyed-nurses-consider-leaving-direct-patient -care-at-elevated-rates.

35. Ranu Sewdas, Astrid de Wind, Sari Stenholm, Pieter Coenen, Ilse Louwerse, Cecile Boot, and Allard van der Beek, "Association between Retirement and Mortality: Working Longer, Living Longer? A Systematic Review and Meta-Analysis," *Journal of Epidemiology and Community Health* 74 (2020): 473–480.

36. Mazzonna Fabrizio and Franco Peracchi, "Unhealthy Retirement?," *Journal of Human Resources* 51, no. 1 (2016): 128–151.

37. Milena Nikolova and Carol Graham, "Employment, Late-Life Work, Retirement, and Well-Being in Europe and the United States," *IZA Journal of European Labor Studies* 3, no. 5 (2014): 1–30.

38. US Department of Labor, Bureau of Labor Statistics, "Quits Rate of 2.9 Percent in August 2021 an All-Time High," *Economics Daily*, October 18, 2021, https://www.bls.gov/opub/ted/2021/quits-rate-of-2-9-percent-in-august-2021 -an-all-time-high.htm.

39. US Department of Labor, Bureau of Labor Statistics, "Empirical Evidence for the 'Great Resignation,'" *Monthly Labor Review*, November 2022, https://doi .org/10.21916/mlr.2022.29.

40. Gallup, *State of the Global Workplace: 2022 Report*, May 2, 2023, https://www .cca-global.com/content/latest/article/2023/05/state-of-the-global-workplace -2022-report-346/.

41. Susan Lund, Anu Madgavkar, James Manyika, Sven Smit, Kweilin Ellingrud, Mary Meaney, and Olivia Robinson, *The Postpandemic Economy: The Future of Work after COVID-19*, McKinsey Global Institute, February 18, 2021, https:// www.mckinsey.com/featured-insights/future-of-work/the-future-of-work-after -covid-19.

42. Lund et al., *The Postpandemic Economy*.

CHAPTER 5

1. American Psychological Association, "Workers Appreciate and Seek Mental Health Support in the Workplace: APA's 2022 Work and Well-Being Survey Results," accessed May 23, 2023, https://www.apa.org/pubs/reports/work -well-being/2022-mental-health-support.

2. Mariella Miraglia and Gary Johns, "Going to Work Ill: A Meta-Analysis of the Correlates of Presenteeism and a Dual-Path Model," *Journal of Occupational Health Psychology* 21, no. 3 (2016): 261–283.

3. Paul Hemp, "Presenteeism: At Work—But Out of It," *Harvard Business Review* 82 (2004): 49–58.

4. Juliet Hassard, Kevin R. Teoh, Gintare Visockaite, Philip Dewe, and Tom Cox, "The Cost of Work-Related Stress to Society: A Systematic Review," *Journal of Occupational Health Psychology* 23, no. 1 (2018): 1–17.

5. Walter F. Stewart, Judith A. Ricci, Elsbeth Chee, David Morganstein, and Richard Lipton, "Lost Productive Rime and Cost Due to Common Pain Conditions in the US Workforce," *Journal of the American Medical Association* 290, no. 18 (2003): 2443–2454.

6. Amy Edmondson, *The Fearless Organization: Creating Psychological Safety in the Workplace for Learning, Innovation, and Growth* (Hoboken: John Wiley and Sons, 2019).

7. Amy C. Edmondson and Derrick P. Bransby, "Psychological Safety Comes of Age: Observed Themes in an Established Literature," *Annual Review of Organizational Psychology and Organizational Behavior* 10 (2023): 55–78.

8. Robert Karasek and Tores Theorell, *Healthy Work: Stress, Productivity, and the Reconstruction of Working Life* (New York: Basic Books, 1990), 312.

9. Hans Selye, "Stress and Disease," *Science* 122, no. 3171 (1995): 625–631.

10. Wan-Chin Kuo, Lisa C. Bratzke, Linda D. Oakley, Fanglin Kuo, Haocen Wang, and Roger L. Brown, "The Association between Psychological Stress and Metabolic Syndrome: A Systematic Review and Meta-Analysis," *Obesity Reviews* 20 (2019): 1651–1664.

11. Tarani Chandola, Eric Brunner, and Michael Marmot, "Chronic Stress at Work and the Metabolic Syndrome: Prospective Study," *BMJ* 332, no. 7540 (2006): 521–525.

12. Karasek and Theorell. *Healthy Work.*

13. Karasek and Theorell, *Healthy Work.*

14. Robert A. Karasek, "Job Demands, Job Decision Latitude, and Mental Strain: Implications for Job Redesign," *Administrative Science Quarterly* 24, no. 2 (1979): 285–308.

15. Jeffrey V. Johnson and Ellen M. Hall, "Job Strain, Work Place Social Support, and Cardiovascular Disease: A Cross-Sectional Study of a Random Sample of the Swedish Working Population," *American Journal of Public Health* 78, no. 10 (1988): 1336–1342.

16. Tino Lesener, Burkhard Guys, and Christine Wolter, "The Job Demands-Resources Model: A Meta-Analytic Review of Longitudinal Studies," *Work and Stress* 33, no. 1 (2019): 76–103; Evangelia Demerouti, Arnold Bakker, Friedhelm Nachreiner, and Wilmar B. Schaufeli, "The Job Demands-Resources Model of Burnout," *Journal of Applied Psychology* 86 (2001): 499–512.

17. Peter Schnall, Marnie Dobson, Ellen Rosskam, and Ray Elling, *Unhealthy Work: Causes, Consequences, Cures* (Amityville, NY: Baywood Publishing Company, 2009).

18. Frederick T. Winslow, *The Principles of Scientific Management*, rev. ed. (1911; repr., Eastford, CT: Martino Fine Books, 2014).

19. Karasek, "Job Demands, Job Decision Latitude, and Mental Strain."

20. Jeffrey Pfeffer, *Dying for a Paycheck: How Modern Management Harms Employee Health and Company Performance—And What We Can Do About It* (New York: Harper Collins, 2018).

21. Centers for Disease Control and Prevention, National Institute for Occupational Safety and Health, *Commercial Fishing Fatality Summary: East Coast Region*, July 17, 2017, https://www.cdc.gov/niosh/docs/2017-173/pdf/2017-173.pdf?id =10.26616/NIOSHPUB2017173; US Coast Guard, Office of Investigations and Analysis, *Analysis of Fishing Vessel Casualties: A Review of Lost Fishing Vessels and Crew Fatalities, 1992–2007*, October 2008, https://www.dco.uscg.mil/Portals/9 /DCO%20Documents/5p/CG-5PC/CG-CVC/CVC3/reports/2008_Casualty _Analysis.pdf.

22. Karasek, "Job Demands, Job Decision Latitude, and Mental Strain: Implications for Job Redesign."

23. Jolanda Hessels, Cornelius A. Rietveld, and Peter van der Zwan, "Self-Employment and Work-Related Stress: The Mediating Role of Job Control and Job Demand," *Journal of Business Venturing* 32, no. 2 (2017): 178–196.

24. Schnall et al., *Unhealthy Work*; Karasek and Theorell, *Healthy Work*.

25. Isabelle Niedhammer, Sandrine Bertrais, and Katrina Witt, "Psychosocial Work Exposures and Health Outcomes: A Meta-Review of 72 Literature Reviews with Meta-Analysis," *Scandinavian Journal of Work Environment and Health* 47, no. 7 (2021): 489–508.

26. Yamna Taouk, Matthew J. Spittal, Anthony D. LaMontagne, and Allison J. Milner, "Psychosocial Work Stressors and Risk of All-Cause and Coronary Heart Disease Mortality: A Systematic Review and Meta-Analysis," *Scandinavian Journal of Work Environment and Health* 42, no. 1 (2020): 19–31.

27. Gabriele Buruck, Anne Tomaschek, Johannes Wendsche, Elke Ochsmann, and Denise Dorfel, "Psychosocial Areas of Worklife and Chronic Low Back Pain: A

Systematic Review and Meta-Analysis," *BMC Musculoskeletal Disorders* 20, no. 480 (2019): 1–16.

28. S. Amiri and S. Behnezhad, "Association between Job Strain and Sick Leave: A Systematic Review and Meta-Analysis of Prospective Cohort Studies," *Public Health* 185 (2020): 235–242.

29. Caroline S. Duchaine , Karine Aube, Mahee Gilbert-Oulmet, Michel Vezina, Ruth Ndjaboue, Victoria Massamba, Denis Talbot, et al., "Psychological Stressors at Work and the Risk of Sickness Absence Due to a Diagnosed Mental Disorder: A Systematic Review and Meta-Analysis," *JAMA Psychiatry* 77, no. 8 (2020): 842–851.

30. Allison Milner, Anna J. Scovelle, Tania L. King, and Ida Madsen, "Exposure to Work Stress and Use of Psychotropic Medications: A Systematic Review and Meta-Analysis," *Journal of Epidemiology and Community Health* 73 (2019): 569–576.

31. Joel Goh, Jeffrey Pfeffer, and Stefanos Zenios, "The Relationship between Workplace Stressors and Mortality and Health Costs in the United States," *Management Science* 62, no. 2 (2016): 608–628; Joel Goh, Jeffrey Pfeffer, and Stefanos Zenios, "Workplace Stressors and Health Outcomes: Health Policy for the Workplace," *Behavioral Science and Policy* 1, no. 1 (2015): 43–52.

32. Pfeffer, *Dying for a Paycheck*.

33. Paul Glavin and Scott Schieman, "Dependency and Hardship in the Gig Economy: The Mental Health Consequences of Platform Work," *Socius: Sociological Research for a Dynamic World* 8 (2022): 1–13.

34. World Health Organization, "Burnout an 'Occupational Phenomenon': International Classification of Diseases," May 28, 2019, https://www.who.int/news /item/28-05-2019-burn-out-an-occupational-phenomenon-international-classifi cation-of-diseases.

35. Christina Maslach and Michael P. Leiter, "Understanding the Burnout Experience: Recent Research and Its Implications for Psychiatry," *World Psychiatry* 15 (2016): 103–111.

36. Christina Maslach, *Burnout: The Cost of Caring* (Englewood Cliffs, NJ: Prentice-Hall, 1982).

37. Maslach and Leiter, "Understanding the Burnout Experience."

38. Christina Maslach, Wilmar B. Schaufeli, and Michael P. Leiter, "Job Burnout," *Annual Review of Psychology* 52 (2001): 397–422; Maslach and Leiter, "Understanding the Burnout Experience."

39. Rohit B. Sangal, Amy Wresniewski, Julia DiBenigno, Elanor Reid, Andrew Ulrich, Beth Liebhardt, Alexandra Bray, et al., "Work Team Identification Associated with Less Stress and Burnout among Front-Line Emergency Department Staff amid the COVID-19 Pandemic," *BMJ Leader* 5 (2021): 51–54.

40. Maslach, Schaufeli, and Leiter, "Job Burnout."

41. US Surgeon General, *Addressing Health Worker Burnout: The US Surgeon General's Advisory on Building a Thriving Health Workforce*, 2022, https://www.hhs.gov /sites/default/files/health-worker-wellbeing-advisory.pdf.

42. Arnold B. Bakker and Juriena D. de Vries, "Job Demands-Resources Theory and Self-regulation: New Explanations and Remedies for Job Burnout," *Anxiety, Stress, and Coping* 34, no. 1 (2021): 1–21.

43. Bakker and de Vries, "Job Demands-Resources Theory and Self-Regulation"; Marianne Borritz, Ute Bultmann, Reiner Rugulies, Karl B. Christensen, Ebbe Villadsen, and Tage S. Kristensen, "Psychosocial Work Characteristics as Predictors for Burnout: Findings from 3-Year Follow Up of the PUMA Study," *Journal of Occupational and Environmental Medicine* 47, no. 10 (2005): 1015–1025.

44. Erin L. Kelly, Lisa F. Berkman, Laura D. Kubzansky, and Meg Lovejoy, "7 Strategies to Improve Your Employees' Health and Well-Being," *Harvard Business Review*, October 12, 2021, https://hbr.org/2021/10/7-strategies-to-improve-your -employees-health-and-well-being.

45. Meg Lovejoy, Erin L. Kelly, Laura D. Kubzansky, and Lisa F. Berkman, "Work Redesign for the 21st Century: Promising Strategies for Enhancing Worker Well-Being," *American Journal of Public Health* 111, no. 10 (2021): 1787–1795.

46. Kimberly E. Fox, Sydney T. Johnson, Lisa F. Berkman, Marjaana Sianoja, Yenee Soh, Laura D. Kubzansky, and Erin L. Kelly, "Organisational- and Group-Level Workplace Interventions and Their Effect on Multiple Domains of Worker Well-Being: A Systematic Review," *Work and Stress* 36, no. 1 (2022): 30–59.

47. Zirui Song and Katherine Baicker, "Effect of a Workplace Wellness Program on Employee Health and Economic Outcomes: A Randomized Clinical Trial," *Journal of the American Medical Association* 321, no. 15 (2019): 1491–1501.

48. Ben Laker, Charmi Patel, Pawan Budhwar, and Ashish Malik, "How Job Crafting Can Make Work More Satisfying," *MIT Sloan Management Review* (September 2020), https://sloanreview.mit.edu/article/how-job-crafting-can-make -work-more-satisfying/.

49. Benn Laker, "What Does the Four-Day Workweek Mean for the Future of Work?," *MIT Sloan Management Review*, May 2022, https://sloanreview.mit.edu /article/what-does-the-four-day-workweek-mean-for-the-future-of-work/.

50. Mind Share Partners, *2021 Mental Health at Work Report*, 2021, https://www .mindsharepartners.org/mentalhealthatworkreport-2021.

51. US Surgeon General, *The US Surgeon General's Framework for Workplace Mental Health and Well-Being*, 2022, https://www.hhs.gov/sites/default/files/workplace -mental-health-well-being.pdf.

52. Sulmaz Ghahramani, Kamran B. Lankarani, Mohammad Yousefi, Keyvan Heydari, Saeed Shahabi, and Sajjad Azmand, "A Systematic Review and Meta-Analysis of Burnout among Healthcare Workers during COVID-19," *Frontiers in Psychiatry* 12 (2021): 758849.

53. Dana R. Garfin, Lindita Djokovic, Roxane C. Silver, and E. Alison Holman, "Acute Stress, Worry, and Impairment in Health Care and Non-Health Care Essential Workers during the COVID-19 Pandemic," *Psychological Trauma* 14, no. 8 (2022): 1304–1313.

54. Gretchen Berlin, Meredith Lapointe, and Mhoire Murphy, "Surveyed Nurses Consider Leaving Direct Patient Care at Elevated Rates," McKinsey and Company, February 17, 2022, https://www.mckinsey.com/industries/healthcare-systems-and-services/our-insights/surveyed-nurses-consider-leaving-direct-patient-care-at-elevated-rates.

55. Massachusetts Health Policy Commission, *Health Care Workforce Trends and Challenges in the Era of COVID-19: Current Outlook and Policy Considerations for Massachusetts* (Boston, MA: Massachusetts Health Policy Commission, 2023), https://www.mass.gov/doc/health-care-workforce-trends-and-challenges-in-the-era-of-covid-19/download.

56. US Department of Labor, Bureau of Labor Statistics, *Occupational Outlook Handbook*, accessed May 23, 2023, https://www.bls.gov/ooh/.

57. Lynda Gratton, *Redesigning Work: How to Transform Your Organization and Make Hybrid Work for Everyone* (Cambridge, MA: MIT Press, 2022).

INDEX

The letter *t* following a page number denotes a table; the letter *f* following a page number denotes a figure.

Absenteeism. *See also* Presenteeism
  performance pay and, 23
  work factors contributing to, 29–30
Accomplishment, lack of, 109, 115
"Active" jobs, 102, 106
Adaptation/adaptability, 51–52, 65
Affective well-being, 47, 49, 74–75, 91
Affordable Care Act, 67
Age differences
  COVID-19 pandemic's impact and,
    69–70
  gig work and, 26
  job satisfaction and, 52, 53, 54–55
  low-skilled workers and, 120
  reduced physicality of labor and, 92
  self-employed workers and, 67
  work-to-family spillover and, 34
Air pollution, 17–18, 60–61, 63, 64f,
  69
Alcohol use, 23, 61–62, 63, 70, 101,
  120
Ali, Muhammad, 11
Allen, Tammy, 35
Allostasis, 101
Alzheimer's disease, 42, 76
Amazon, 68
American Psychological Association,
  98
American School Sisters of Notre
  Dame, 42
Antianxiety medications, 23

Antidepressants, 23
Anxiety
  COVID-19 pandemic and, 112–113
  job insecurity and, 107
  job satisfaction and, 52–53
  psychological safety and, 99–100
  underemployment and, 65
  work factors contributing to, 29
Ariely, Dan, 45
Aristotle, 75
Artificial intelligence, 91–92
Atypical working hours, 31–32, 34, 38
Automation, 91–92
Autonomic nervous system (ANS),
  100–101
Autonomy, 102, 106, 111

Back pain, chronic, 107
Behavioral economics, 45, 46
Berg, Justin, 53
BF Goodrich, 57–58
Bimodel earnings distribution, 66
BJ's, 112
Bob (fisher). *See also* Commercial
  fishing
  description of job of, 117
  economic theory and, 45–46
  interview with, 127–128
  introduction to, 1–3
  meaningful work and, 89–90
  risk and, 105, 106

Boredom, 86–87
Borjas, George, 52, 67–68
Budget constraints, 44
"Bullshit jobs," 87
Bureau of Labor Statistics (BLS), 2, 6,
    19, 24–25, 68, 90, 114
Burnout
    COVID-19 pandemic and, 112–114
    disengagement and, 7
    drug enforcement job and, 13–14, 30
    general discussion of, 108–114
    impact of, 126
    job satisfaction and, 53
    job strain model and, 103
    low job control and, 29
    managing, 111–112
    meaningless work and, 87
    remote work options and, 123
    stress and, 8
    unions and, 68

Cancer
    diesel exhaust and, 60–61
    night shift work and, 31
Card, David, 53
Center for Applied Research in the
    Apostolate, 79
Challenges, 86t
Cheryl (insurance agent), 95–100,
    105–107, 108, 115, 117
Childbirth, mortality risk and, 78
Childcare obligations, 36, 38
Choice, importance of, 70
Chronic health effects, 17, 19–20
Chronic job strain, 107–108
Chronic stress, 106
Circadian rhythm, 32
Collective myopia, 6
Commercial fishing. See also Bob
    (fisher)
    introduction to, 1–4
    lack of safety measures and, 22
    as most dangerous occupation, 2

rational choice theory and, 45
retirement and, 89
risks of, 14–15, 16, 105
"Common sense" approach to safety,
    46
Communication patterns, changes in,
    36
Commute time, 35, 38, 122–123
Compensating wage differentials, 20
Compensation. See Salary/
    compensation
Concentration camps, 75, 76
Consumption, utility models and, 51
Contemplative nuns, 77
Contingent work, 30
Control
    lack of, 28–30, 34
    shift of back to workers, 111
COVID-19 pandemic
    burnout and, 110
    gig work and, 27
    Great Resignation and, 6–7
    impact of, 8, 19–20, 37, 38, 69–70,
        71, 91
    meaningful work and, 87–88, 90–
        92, 93
    remote work and, 34–35
    self-employed workers and, 66
    stress and burnout and, 112–114
    underemployment and, 65
Creativity, communication patterns
    and, 36

Dalai Lama, 59
Darlene (supervisor), 73–74, 89–90,
    117
Death rates
    decrease in, 18
    low job control and, 107–108
    opioid use and, 17
    recessions and, 61
    suicide rates, 61, 70, 120
Deaths of despair, 61–62, 70, 120

Deaton, Angus, 49
Decision theory, 45
Depersonalization, 109
Depression
  burnout versus, 110
  COVID-19 pandemic and, 112–113
  genetics and, 43
  high job demand and, 107
  job insecurity and, 107
  job satisfaction and, 53
  Lincoln and, 47
  long working hours and, 107
  underemployment and, 65
  work factors contributing to, 29
Detachment, 109, 115
De-unionization efforts, 62
Diabetes, 31, 67, 101, 107
Diesel exhaust, 60–61, 63. *See also* Air pollution
Diminishing marginal utility, 44
Disaffected workers, 86–87
Disengagement, 7, 113
Distrust, culture of, 99
Drug enforcement job, 12–14, 27–29, 31, 81–82, 108–110, 117
Drug use, recreational, 23, 61–62, 63, 70, 120
Dual growth mindset, 53–54

Earthquake, in Haiti, 21
Easterlin, Richard, 47–48
Easterlin Paradox, 48, 51, 54
E-commerce, 91–92
Economic utility theory, 47–48
Edmondson, Amy, 99–100
Education, nuns and, 78
Education levels
  COVID-19 pandemic's impact and, 69
  gender differences and, 36
  low-skilled workers and, 120
  mortality rates and, 62, 70

reduced physicality of labor and, 92
self-employed workers and, 66–67
Efficiency management, 103–104, 123–124
Effort-reward imbalance, 103, 107, 110, 115
Electronic monitoring, 98, 104, 113, 115
Emotional exhaustion, 109, 115
Emotionally draining work, 113
Employment mobility, 52
Ergonomic stressors, 35, 38–39, 123
Eudaemonic well-being, 47, 74–76, 88, 91, 92–93
Evaluative well-being, 47, 74–75, 91
Exercise, 63, 101
Existential labor, 87

Factor analytic techniques, 83
Family responsibilities. *See also* Work-life balance
  conflicts with, 34
  remote work options and, 35
Fatalism, 3
Fatigue, 28
Fatigue mats, 18
Federal Law Enforcement Training Center (FLETC), 12
Feedback, lack of, 110
Female labor force participation, 79–80, 79f
Feminization of workforce, 26–27, 38
Fight-or-flight response, 100, 101–102
Flexibility
  burnout and, 111
  employee empowerment and, 38
  remote work options and, 35, 99, 122, 123
Four-day work week, 112
Franciscan Children's hospital, 78
Franciscan Sisters of Mary, 78
Frankl, Viktor, 73, 75, 76
Freeman, Richard, 52

Gallup-Healthways Well-Being Index, 49
Gallup World Poll, 50, 66, 88–89, 90–91
GAP, 34
Gender differences
  changes in, 38–39
  COVID-19 pandemic and, 20, 69
  drug enforcement and, 81–82
  education levels and, 36
  female labor force participation and, 79–80, 79f
  feminization of workforce and, 26–27, 38
  historical, 118–119
  job satisfaction and, 52, 53, 54
  low-skilled workers and, 120
  reduced physicality of labor and, 92
  remote work options and, 35, 36
  risk aversion and, 16
  work-to-family spillover and, 34
Gender wage gap, 26
General adaptation syndrome, 101
Genetics, happiness and, 43, 44
Geographic differences, self-employed workers and, 67
Gig pay/work. See also Performance pay
  atypical working hours and, 34
  efficiency management and, 104
  feminization of workforce, 26–27, 38
  impact of, 24–26, 30–31, 37, 119
  job stress and, 108
  pay structure and, 20–24
Goh, Joel, 107–108
Graeber, David, 87
Gratton, Lynda, 114
Great Recession, 65, 90
Great Resignation, 6, 90–91, 120, 121
Group belonging, 110
Growth mindset, 53–54

Habituation, 51
Haiti, earthquake in, 21
Hammond, Tom, 15
Happiness
  Aristotle on, 75
  comparison and, 53, 54
  dual growth mindset and, 53–54
  economic theories on, 43–44
  genetics and, 43, 44
  income levels and, 4–5, 48–49, 48f, 50t, 54
  inequality and, 51
  job satisfaction and, 52–54
  longevity and, 42–43, 42t, 54
  measuring, 46–47
  money and, 47–52, 127
  nature versus nurture and, 43, 44
  nun study and, 41–43, 42t
  questions asked regarding, 7
  underemployment and, 65
  unemployment and, 64–65
Harknett, Kristen, 33
Health. See also Mental health; Well-being
  cancer and, 31, 60–61
  chronic health effects, 17, 19–20
  chronic pain, 16
  diabetes, 31, 67, 101, 107
  exercise, 63, 101
  heart disease, 31, 98, 101, 102, 107, 113, 124
  meaningful work and, 76
  recessions and, 60–63
  retirement and, 88–89
  sick leave/sick time, 62, 97–98, 99, 107, 115
  strokes, 76, 101, 107
  workplace wellness programs, 112
Health insurance
  gig work and, 25, 27
  lack of, 16
  management strategies and, 126

self-employed workers and, 67
unionization and, 68
Heart disease, 31, 98, 101, 102, 107, 113, 124
Heart rate, performance pay and, 23
Hedonic treadmill, 51–52, 54, 55
Hedonic wage function, 20
Hedonic well-being, 47
High job demand, 29, 102, 107–108, 110
Hutchinson, Christopher, 14–15, 16–17
Hybrid work options, 35, 36, 39, 124
Hypothermia, 15

Idea generation, communication patterns and, 36
Idle time policies, 96–98, 103, 104, 124, 125
Incentive (performance) pay, 20–24
Inclusivity, 110
Income levels. See Salary/compensation
Income precarity, 108
Incorporated self-employment, 66
Independent contractors, 25
Industrial engineering, 103
Industrial hygiene, 18
Ineffectiveness, sense of, 109
Inequality, happiness and, 51
Inequities in labor market, worsening of, 7
Inflammation
happiness and, 43
performance pay and, 23
Inner self, developing, 83
International Agency for Research on Cancer, 31, 60
Interpersonal interactions, meaningful work and, 85
Irrational choices, 45
Isolation
remote work options and, 35, 38
Taylorism and, 103

Job crafting, 112
Job-demand-control model, 29–30, 102, 108, 124
Job-demand-control-support model, 102, 109
Job design factors, meaningful work and, 84, 84t
Job insecurity, 34, 107
Jobs
history of, 4
siloed approach to study of, 6
Job satisfaction
happiness and, 52–54
remote work and, 35–36, 39
self-employed workers and, 66–67
unionization and, 67–68, 71
Job strain, chronic, 107–108
Job strain model, 99, 102–103, 106–107, 109, 115
Journal of the American Medical Association, 112

Kahneman, Daniel, 49
Karasek, Robert, 100, 102, 104, 106
Katz, Lawrence, 25
Kelly, Erin, 111–112
Kennedy, Joseph and Rose, 78
Killingsworth, Matthew, 49
Klotz, Anthony, 6
Krueger, Alan, 25

Labor mobility, increased, 27
Laker, Ben, 112
Latin American countries, happiness and, 50
Leadership and management factors, meaningful work and, 84, 84t
Learned helplessness, 46, 111
Life, meaningful, 74–76
Life satisfaction, 47, 49
Lifespan/life expectancy
happiness and, 42–43, 42t, 54
meaningful work and, 76, 78–79, 93

Lifespan/life expectancy (cont.)
  nuns and, 78
  retirement and, 88
Lincoln, Abraham, 47
Lobster industry, 14–15
Loss, responses to, 65
Low job control, 28–30, 34, 38, 102, 107–108, 110
Low-skilled opportunities, disappearance of, 119–120
Lung cancer, 60–61

Maine, commercial fishing in. *See* Bob (fisher); Commercial fishing
Maine Marine Patrol, 15
Marine Patrol, 1
Maslach, Christina, 109
Maslach Burnout Inventory, 109, 113–114
Maslow's hierarchy of needs, 77
McKinsey Global Institute, 69
Meaningful life, 74–76
Meaningful work
  COVID-19 pandemic and, 90–92
  defining, 76–77
  drivers of, 86t
  experience of over time, 87–88
  interdisciplinary study of, 80–85
  introduction to, 73–74
  meaningful life and, 74–76
  meaningless work versus, 85–87
  nuns and, 77–80
  predictors of, 83–84, 84t
  questions asked regarding, 7–8
  resilience and, 120–121
  retirement and, 88–90
  review of, 117
  summary regarding, 92–93
Mental health
  compensation and, 30
  COVID-19 pandemic and, 112–113
  job satisfaction and, 52–53
  job stress and, 107

psychological safety and, 99–100
  unionization and, 68
  work factors contributing to, 29
Mental strain, 102–103, 104
Metabolic syndrome, 101, 102, 107, 113
Micromanagement, 99, 106, 113, 115, 124. *See also* Tracking of employees
Microsoft, 36
Mill, John S., 51–52
"Monday blues," 52, 55
Mood, measures of, 47
Mortality rates
  deaths of despair and, 61–62, 70, 120
  decrease in, 18
  education levels and, 62, 70
  low job control and, 107–108
  opioid use and, 17, 62
  recessions and, 61
  suicide rates, 61, 70, 120

"National efficiency" crisis, 103
National Institute for Occupational Safety and Health, 18
National Labor Relations Board, 68
Nature versus nurture, 41–43
Nicomachean Ethics (Aristotle), 75
Nietzsche, Friedrich, 117
Night shift work, 31–33
No Limits (lobster boat), 14–15, 16, 17, 37
North American Sisters, 41–42
Nuns
  autobiographical statements from, 41–42, 47
  labor force participation rates and, 79–80, 79f, 93
  meaningful work and, 77–80, 117
Nun Study of Aging and Alzheimer's Disease, 42, 77, 78
Nurse practitioners, 114
Nurses, 87–88, 91, 110, 113–114

Obesity
  high job demand and, 107
  night shift work and, 32
  recessions and, 61
Occupational Safe and Health Act (1970), 104
Occupational Safety and Health Administration, 126
Online gig platforms, 24–26
Opioid use
  mortality rates and, 17, 62
  physically demanding jobs and, 16–17
Opportunity entrepreneurs, 66–67
Organizational change, 30
Organizational factors, meaningful work and, 84, 84t, 86t
Organizations
  meaningful work and, 85, 93
  meaningless work and, 85–86, 86t, 93
Organization size, job satisfaction and, 52

Paid time off (PTO), 97–98
Pain, chronic, 16
Pandemic. See COVID-19 pandemic
Paradox of the Contented Female Worker, 53
Parenthood, risk aversion and, 16
Part-time work, 30–31
Pay structure, 20–23
"People work," stress of, 109
Performance pay, 20–24, 30, 34, 37. See also Gig pay/work
Personal drivers of meaningful work, 86t
Pew Research Center, 25
Physical hazards, reduction in, 104–105
Physicality of work, 118, 123, 125
Piece rate, 20–24. See also Gig pay/ work; Performance pay

Pink-collar workers, 85
Platform-dependent workers, 25–26, 108, 119
Polaroid, 59–60
Potential, expressing full, 83
Poverty, happiness and, 5, 49, 51
Powerlessness, 28
Precarious work, 30
Presenteeism, 99, 113, 115, 124, 126. See also Absenteeism
Principles of Scientific Management, The (Taylor), 103
Profits, irregular scheduling's impact on, 34
Psychological safety, 99–100
Psychosocial workplace hazards, 104–107, 126

Quiet quitting, 7, 113, 126
Quit rates, 6, 90, 91

Racial disparities
  COVID-19 pandemic and, 19, 20, 69
  essential workers and, 118
  gig work and, 26
  low-skilled workers and, 120
  reduced physicality of labor and, 92
Rational choice theory, 45–46
Rationality, importance of, 45–46
Recessions, health and, 60–63
Reckless behavior, 16, 17
Redesigning Work (Gratton), 114
Reflection, 86t
Remote work
  COVID-19 pandemic and, 34–36
  impact of, 38–39
  job satisfaction and, 35–36, 39
  job stress and, 95–99, 113
  labor mobility and, 27
  meaningful work and, 91–92, 93
  pros and cons of, 122–124
  turnover and, 35, 123

Resignation risk, increased, 69–70, 90
Resilience, 65, 120–121
Retirement, 88–90, 121–122
Risks. *See also* Safety protocols, lack of compliance with
    income and, 45
    individual characteristics and, 17
    lack of recognition of, 46
    Maine fishers and, 1–3, 15, 16
    perceptions of, 2–3, 7, 15, 46
    rational choice theory and, 45–46
    work-related factors and, 18
Role, meaningful work and, 85
Role ambiguity, 110
Role conflict, 110
Ruhm, Christopher, 61

Sadler, Michael E., 43
Safety protocols. *See also* Risks
    lack of compliance with, 2, 15, 21–22, 46, 105
Safety suits, 15
Salary/compensation
    comparison and, 53, 55
    derivation of word, 4
    gender differences and, 53, 54
    gender wage gap and, 26
    happiness and, 44, 48–49, 48f, 50t, 54, 127
    higher income levels and, 4–5
    importance of, 20
    job satisfaction and, 52, 53
    mental health and, 30
    safety versus, 21–22
    self-employed workers and, 66
    unionization and, 67–68
    worker health and, 20–23
Salt, as currency, 4
Sandy (Cheryl's friend), 97–98, 99
Saturation point, 49
Sawyer, Tyler, 15

Schedules, low level of control over, 27, 29. *See also* Atypical working hours
Schneider, Daniel, 33
Schor, Juliet, 25
Scientific management, 103–104, 123–124, 125–126
Seaman's manslaughter, 16
Self-employed workers, 26, 66–67, 70, 89, 106, 121, 122
Self-transcendence, 77, 86t
Selye, Hans, 100–101
Serving others, 83
Set point theory, 64
Shift Project, 33
Shift work, 31–33. *See also* Atypical working hours
Shoes, musculoskeletal problems and, 18
Sick leave/sick time, 62, 97–98, 99, 107, 115
Sleep, stable scheduling intervention and, 34
Smith, Adam, 41, 95
Smoking, air quality and, 17–18
Snowdon, David, 41–42
Social media, happiness and, 52
Social networks, happiness and, 50, 54
Social pollution, 104
Social supports, 30, 102, 104, 123. *See also* Support
Sorensen, Glorian, 18
Stable scheduling intervention, 34, 125
Starbucks, 68
Stress
    chronic, 106
    COVID-19 pandemic and, 112–113
    economic downturns and, 62
    effects of long-term exposure to, 101
    happiness and, 43
    micromanagement and, 99
    performance pay and, 23
    physiology of, 100–102

psychological safety and, 99–100
recessions and, 63
in workplace, 102–108
work-related, 8
Strokes, 76, 101, 107
Suicide rates, 61, 70, 120
Sunlight, 32
Support
increase in, 112
lack of, 110
Sweatshops, 18, 21–22

Tasks, meaningful work and, 85
Task surveillance, 113, 115, 124, 125
Taylor, Frederick, 103–104
Taylorism, 103–104
Temporary workers, 24–25, 30
Theorell, Töres, 100
Threshold theory of income and
happiness, 49
Tools, history of, 4
Total Worker Health initiatives, 18–19,
126
Tracking of employees, 96–98, 99,
104. See also Micromanagement
Trivialism, 3–4
Truck drivers, air quality and, 17–18,
60–61
Trucking Industry Particle Study
(TrIPS), 60–61
Truman, Harry S., 57
Turnover
boredom and, 92
impact of, 126
job satisfaction and, 52
meaningless work and, 87
remote work and, 35, 123
Twin study on happiness, 43

Underemployment, 65–66, 70
Unemployment
air pollution and, 64f
COVID-19 pandemic and, 69

happiness and, 64–65
impact of, 63, 70
well-being and, 64–66
Unionization, 52, 62, 67–68, 70–71,
121, 122
Unity with others, 83
University of California system, salary
disclosure and, 53
Ursuline sisters, 77
US Census Bureau, 34–35
US Customs Service, 11–13, 31
US Surgeon General, 110, 113
Utility, 44, 51. See also Happiness

Values, misalignment in, 82, 86, 86t,
110
Videoconferencing, 36
Vieira, Alice, 57–60, 58f, 59f, 117
Vitamin D, 32

Well-being. See also Health; Mental
health
affective, 47, 49, 74–75, 91
efforts to improve, 111–112
employment and, 60–71
eudaemonic, 47, 74–76, 88, 91,
92–93
evaluative, 47, 74–75, 91
happiness and, 47
opportunistically self-employed and,
66–67
recessions and, 70
underemployment and, 65–66
unionization and, 68
Wellness programs, 126
Worker control, erosion of, 103–104
Work-life balance
atypical working hours and, 33–
34
job stress and, 113
meaningful work and, 84t, 85
remote work and, 35, 36–37, 38,
122–123, 124

Work overload, 110
Workplace injuries and illnesses, rates
    of, 18. *See also* Health; Risks
Workplace interventions, 112
Workplace relationship factors,
    meaningful work and, 84–85, 84t
Workplace wellness programs, 112
Work schedule
  atypical, 31–32
  inconsistent, 31, 33–34
Work-to-family spillover, 34, 35–36
World Health Organization, 19, 109

Zero-tolerance policies, 28